Seeking True North

The Pathway to Freedom, Beauty and Success

Erick Erickson & Tim Walther

"SEEKING TRUE NORTH" • © 2008 • ISBN#9 780974 628844

SEEKING TRUE NORTH

Editing by Vanessa Sands, Marian Buda, Jamie Reilly
and the Seeking True North Readers Group.

Cover by Charlie Ritchie and Catherine Coe

Graphics by Michelle Bevier

Page Layout by James Morrow

Printed-On-Demand by Morrow Graphics, Inc.
in The United States of America

For Telos

Praise for
Seeking True North

"Powerful and practical life success strategies for investing in your most important assets...Read this book and reap the benefits — now!"

> —Phil Town, #1 *New York Times* best-selling author of *Rule # 1*

"There's no 'new truth,' but there are new ways of communicating timeless truth, and this book is proof. The authors tell an interesting story and weave in sound suggestions, advice and techniques. I love the *Seeking True North* tools the book explains, and you will, too. Read it and learn."

> —Mark Sanborn, speaker and author of *The Fred Factor: How Passion in Your Work and Life Can Turn the Ordinary Into the Extraordinary*

"The crisis of our time is wasted human potential. Potential is what we are theoretically capable of doing, but performance is what we are willing to do on any given day, and they often do not match. The key to unlocking human potential is aligning performance with potential, so that we don't just live, but live with impact. This book is about unlocking the power of vision, which fuels drive, which unlocks potential."

> — Dr. Rich Handley, EQ University, co-author of *Optimizing People: A Practical Guide for Applying Emotional Intelligence*

"*Seeking True North* should be required reading for all graduate schools and corporate leadership seminars. I wish it had been around 30 years ago when I was seeking my own life path. Within these pages is a formula for creating a life that is deeply meaningful. Buried within us all is a curiosity about the unknown that we need to pursue. Helen Keller once expressed, "Life can be an exciting adventure — or nothing at all." *Seeking True North* guides us through the ways to discover and develop the courage to act on our passions, enabling us to climb to almost limitless personal and professional summits. It is a guide for figuring out how to find that exciting spirit of adventure within us. And it is a poignant reminder that life is about the journey — not the destination."

> — Al Read, co-owner, Exum Mountain Guides

"This is a simple but powerful story, filled with positive life-changing tools for a much better life and world for each of us. Erickson and Walther are truly 'passing it on.'"

> — Gregory Scott Reid, chief executive officer, Wish Entertainment, creators of the film *Pass It On*

"*Seeking True North* is essential reading for anyone looking for success…whether that means to build a business, find inner peace, increase bliss, create balance or enrich relationships. This book is a manual that helps show us the way to freedom and happiness, and a guide for personal and professional transformation."

> — Mandy Parent, president, Data Net Solutions Group, Inc.

"*Seeking True North* challenges the reader to look deep inside and step out of one's comfort zone to blaze a trail for others to follow. It's a journey beyond the normal leadership realm where you are challenged to expand your parameters and prepare to accomplish things you probably didn't think possible. To fully appreciate the power of this book, read it with an open mind and an open heart. Only then will you find your own True North — and the passion to lead others on that journey we call life."

> — Mike Molaro, director, chapter relations, Construction Financial Management Association

"We are meaning-seeking creatures. However, sometimes we can become complacent in our journey or worse yet…disoriented. *Seeking True North* is a powerful little book, written in fable style, which can put us back on the path that is right for us. It builds the bridge from where we are to where we hope to be -- starting the journey with ourselves and ending with others. I have personally observed the power of the allegory to change the lives of experiential workshop participants who have been exposed to the concept of True North. Pound for pound, this manual packs a powerful punch for the curious "traveler."

— Ron Peckham, executive vice president, The C&S Companies

"We all have that subtle feeling of destiny that Tim and Erick call True North. To excel, to embrace life, to qualify each moment before our own consciousness, we all need transformative experiences and techniques for ongoing self-disciplines to harness the mind and body. *Seeking True North* is a call to excellence, a map for practical progress, and a journey we all must take to become leaders in our lives and fulfill the destiny we each have."

— Gurucharan S. Khalsa, PhD, director of KRI, co-author of *Breathwalk*

Seeking True North guides us as we climb the most challenging mountains of life. Use these tools and you will reach the top of your highest peaks.

— Josh Morris, director, Chiang Mai Rock Climbing Adventures

"The concepts and tools presented in *Seeking True North* have enhanced the quality of my workshops. Erick and Tim creatively weave leadership and personal development skills into an engaging storyline. This book is an interesting read, packed with tools for anyone involved with people-building and teams."

— Tom Gardner, Team Adventure

"*Seeking True North* is a fantastically simple guide to team and business development. On a personal level, it has helped me continue the pursuit of my goals, dreams and quest for happiness! And by the way — I carry my compass in my purse!"

> — Christine LaRocque, sales and events manager, White Mountain Adventures, Banff, Canada

"The experience of Seeking True North and putting the concepts into living has not only created new opportunities, but has led me to a better understanding of the things that are really important in life. This book not only has a great story, but an awesome blueprint for positive change in both your personal and professional worlds. It reminds you to live life to the very fullest, every single day. It is simply AWESOME!"

> — Ann Anderson, vice president of ACE (Awesome Customer Experience), Sallie Mae

"*Seeking True North* creates an experiential learning environment by having you see what participants in a leadership development session experience and learn through a myriad of tools provided by the authors. The tools come alive for you, rather than just being suggestions out of the latest self-help book. Do not overlook the power of these tools. Put them into practice to create a positive, life-changing experience!"

> — Jean Lein, chief financial officer, Haegelin Construction

"What a tremendous and fantastic story of real life, portrayed by the characters Freedom and Beautiful. This story takes us on a life-changing journey, passionately scripted out with the steps necessary to possess amazing growth in our lives. It is a refreshing and brilliant delivery of the tools necessary to bring about a life that will never be same!"

> — Melissa Pinkster, chief financial officer, Consumers Concrete

"Beautiful and Freedom are endearing characters who, through their journey and growth, exposed me to glimpses of myself, be it fear, hope, skepticism, low self esteem or a desire to do more or be more. As I followed along their journey of self-discovery and goal achieving, I realized by preparing and practicing — two major themes shared through these characters' eyes — that I too could take control of my life, attitude, happiness and success. I will read this book again and again as I take my own journey and change my life."

> — Jenni Haines, installation coordinator and training manager for Ritz-Carlton Hotels and Marriott International

"As a trainer, author and facilitator, I found the stories, models, concepts and tools outstandingly accessible to the reader. Tim and Erick have packed more powerful lessons into 100 or so pages than most authors do in 1000. *Seeking True North* invites us to 'raise the bar' for ourselves, pulling us up to an even higher plane, from which the view looks very optimistic indeed."

> — Jim Cain, Ph.D., author of *Teamwork & Teamplay and A Teachable Moment*

Teachers!! Teachers too can benefit from Seeking True North. Just as the trainers in the story used the tips and tools to work with the participants in the "advance" - so too can teachers work with their classroom students. Wisdom and learning can be passed on in many ways, we appreciate how Erick and Tim have shared theirs in this wonderful book.

> — Chris and Susana Cavert - Teachers, Authors, Trainers and Learners.

"There is no magic pill that will transform your life for the better. There is no magic self-help book that will do that, either. This book, however, no matter where you are emotionally, can be your guide for real self-improvement. Erick and Tim have put the tools out on the workbench; you need to grab them and practice using them, and you will see explosive personal growth. Read it, and today you may just have one of the most incredibly awesome days of your entire life."

> — Ed Bradley, chief financial officer, Atlas Services

"*Seeking True North* is a refreshing approach to the balance of internal and external relationships and indoor and outdoor experiences, all in harmony and happiness. Thank you for showing me the way to live the beauty of life and experience the freedom of climbing 'Myself Mountain.'"

— Meira Kober, Ishtar Outdoor Learning, Israel

"Everyone can learn from reading *Seeking True North*. Erick and Tim take an interesting and different approach to focusing on some fundamental truths, which can easily be forgotten in the rushed pace of modern living. Coming from a culture that recognizes the value of meditation in daily living, I was interested and pleased to see that Tim and Erick recommend that people in the West also learn about meditation."

— Prateep Ungsongtham Hata, secretary general, Thailand

"*Seeking True North* is a provocative field guide for the world of corporate motivation. This book provides the models, methods and tools for anyone searching for that "missing link" — both personally and professionally. I read the book, applied the lessons and almost instantly began experiencing positive results! Thank you for leading the way."

— Matt Campana, president, Corporate Motivation, Inc.

"Through reading the story of two main characters that are profoundly changed, you get to share their many 'ah-has' and experience them as if you too attended this powerful life-changing event. The takeaway is a new set of tools and ideas that help empower you to live life more productively and fully. Well, well worth the read."

— Gillian Pierce, international coordinator, Smart Wool

"I know of no other leadership skill development maestros who deliver excellence with a capital E as do Tim Walther and Erick Erickson. The *Seeking True North* experience is a journey filled with adventure, comfort zone expansion and self-exploration you will find nowhere else. Having participated in ongoing True North adventures with Grand Dynamics, my association is living proof that our strong and highly successful leadership culture is a direct result of these incredible journeys. Travel these pages and discover your own True North!"

> — Bill Schwab, president and chief executive officer, Construction Financial Management Association

"Self improvement requires developing self awareness and applying it in one's life. *Seeking True North* can guide you in being aware and taking action."

> — Arno Ilgner, author of *The Rock Warrior's Way: Mental Training for Climbers*

"*Seeking True North* is a winner. You will gain valuable insights, clarified focus and experience a great read!"

> — Don Hutson, CEO of U. S. Learning, and Co-author with Ken Blanchard of *The One Minute Entrepreneur*

"We have been taught that important teachings must be complex and complicated — that for things to have value, they must be hard to explain and hard to understand. Erick and Tim have proven the opposite. They have keenly demonstrated that the Great Truths are not just simple: They are *elegantly* simple. They have taken the meaning and purpose of life and made it elegantly simple so that each of us may find our personal True North. Bravo, gentlemen, bravo."

> — Bill Bartmann, Billionaire Business Coach

Contents

Acknowledgements

The models, methods and tools in this book have come from direct experiences with many friends, teachers, facilitators, business leaders, authors and family members throughout the years of experience of authors Erick Erickson and Tim Walther. While the bibliography references many of these sources, we would also like to acknowledge the following people:

Ann Anderson, Jonathan Benak, Cal Beyer, Jim Cain, Matt Campana, Joey and Dino Denatale, Paul Dickey, Hanie Eng, Andrew Erickson, Edwin and Marie Erickson, Johanna Erickson, Ryan Ernst, Donna Evans, Gary Falk, Scott Fessler, Gavin Fine, Mark Harris, Jenni Haines, Jasper Hunt, Sam and Suchada Johnson, Erik Kampe, Stephen Koch, Gurucharan Khalsa, Tom Leahy, Will Leggett, Mike Molaro, Josh Morris, Justin Musa, Dev Pahtik, Mandy Parent, Ron Peckam, Brian Prax, Jamie Reilly, Charlie Ritchie, Bill Schwab, Jarad Spackman, Mark Tuttle, Todd Walther, Bob Walther and Peg Walther

Foreword

When I read a manuscript, I do it out of obligation to the author, not knowing what to expect but hoping it will be interesting and profitable. *Seeking True North* is one of the most enjoyable reading experiences I've ever had. Reading just a few pages will provoke you to think and to decide if you are a prisoner, vacationer or leader. I had to smile when the authors explain why it is great to lie, cheat or steal.

As you follow the journey of the main characters, Freedom and Beautiful, it is easy to see yourself walking in their footsteps. As they learn life-success strategies from the Older and Younger Facilitators, you begin to realize this journey is really about YOU. Almost every page challenges you to consider a new dimension of an old truth. *Seeking True North* is educational, motivational, challenging, convincing, inspiring and entertaining.

You can read this book in about an hour. You will come back to the principles it teaches for a lifetime. No foreword can do this book justice. It contains so much wisdom, you begin to wonder how they did it. This is a story about living, learning and laughter. It will remain with you the rest of your life.

Thank you, Erick and Tim. I'll never forget the meaning of True North.

Tremendously,
Dr. Charles "Tremendous" Jones

First Introduction

Impact

Every once in a while, you read something that has a major positive impact in your life. Maybe it's a touching story that you can relate to. Maybe it's a concept that has been in your subconscious waiting to surface. Whatever its form, it will be something that leads you toward the destiny you have envisioned. My expectation is that *Seeking True North* will be one of these books for you.

Perspective

You may recognize the picture of the Tetons, in Jackson Hole, Wyoming, on the cover of this book. You may or may not realize that the photograph was actually taken facing west, yet the compass arrow faces north. One day, one of my climber friends looked at the cover and asked, "What's the deal?"

"Here's the deal," I replied. "The picture is a metaphor for our story. The compass is a universal symbol of direction and navigation. *Seeking True North* is about making the pathway through life easier and more fulfilling. To me, the mountains are symbolic of many things, including freedom and beauty. The main characters in our book are named Freedom and Beautiful. Our story is about seeking freedom in our attitude and actions every moment of the day, and living the beauty that life has to offer."

"Whoa! I think I'll read the book!" he replied.

Whom This Book Is For

If you are a leader, manager, teacher or facilitator, this book is for you. If you are an individual seeking to optimize your experience here on planet Earth, this book is for you. It is the culmination of years of experience working with individuals, teams and organizations to address the challenges that matter most. Over the years, "Master Rick" (as I fondly refer to my co-author) and I have facilitated many multi-day corporate retreats together. This is our area of expertise. At the conclusion of each retreat, we stand before our participants to review the insights and applications we have discovered during our time together. These strategy sessions consistently produce an incredible number of personal and professional take-aways. We have been asked on many occasions when we would write a book about it all. Well, here it is!

Evolution

What you are about to read is simple, yet not simplistic. As you will see, the True North model of Prepare, Practice and Passion is one that makes universal sense. It is a process of human evolution in which we all search out ways to "succeed" in life and help others do the same. Each of us may have a different definition of success, but we all have the opportunity to prepare by clarifying and visualizing our desired end results, to practice by seeking models, methods and tools that create success as we define it, to wake up every day excited to be alive and to live a life of passion!

These are the things that I need to know, and the things of which I remind myself every day. If you are ready to experience insights that will have a major, positive impact in your life, then sit back, relax and enjoy our story.

Tim Walther

Second Introduction

Do you ever have a desire to make every day count for good? Do you want more free time to spend with family and friends? Do you want to make more money with less effort and have fun every day? Do you wish having all those great attributes of a quality life were easy and simple?

It can be very simple...with the right tools and systems. Your professional and personal life can be greatly enhanced by choosing the right tools and using them in a consistent manner.

Deep inside, we each long for fulfillment, love and peace in life, and for the means of attaining them. We are not alone in our search for meaning and purpose and for the right vehicles to attain those ends; every human being longs to know the reasons for existing each and every day.

For all of us, *Seeking True North* is a constant, enjoyable pursuit — a process of knocking, asking and learning about who we *sense* we must be. At some point, we must ask ourselves, "What freedom do I want in my life?" and, "What is beautiful to me in life?"

So what is "True North" as we refer to it in this book?

It is known by many names. It is similar to the "meaning" that Viktor Frankl describes in his book, *Man's Search for Meaning*. It resembles what Easterners call "Oneness," and what Pastor Mac at my church calls "The God Hole." It is near to what William W. Woodbridge identifies as "That Something" in his book of the same name.

The "True North" in your life will be unique. *How* you explore the reality of "True North" in your life remains to be discovered. As you will discover in this book, there are many vehicles, tools, models and methods for *Seeking True North*.

My close friends know that a big part of seeking *my* "True North" is something I do every day. Upon waking each morning, I say aloud, "Today is one of the most incredibly awesome days of my entire life."

Some of my friends question, in a positive way, how every day could be the most incredibly awesome day of my entire life. You might question it as well if you were stuck with me for an entire day!

As a third-generation carpenter, I must have many tools in my tool belt and toolbox to use on a variety of building projects. As humans, we need a variety of tools in our *life mastery* tool belts to create more meaningful, effective and productive lives. I trust that you will find at least a few tools within this book that will help you in seeking *your* True North. I can honestly say that the incredible Master Tim Walther and I use all of these tools on a continual basis. The tools work — otherwise, we would toss them! I expect that this book will become instrumental in fostering positive growth in your life.

As a fellow member of the human race, I humbly encourage you to always continue *Seeking True North*.

After you read this book and begin using some of the tools within, I hope our paths will cross and we can share our discoveries for making a positive difference in our lives. I'm sure I will learn something from your sharing.

Meanwhile, I peacefully continue my seeking…

Erick Erickson

How to Use This Book

This book is designed to address multiple learning styles. There are two main parts. Part One is the story of a man named Freedom and a woman named Beautiful. It follows their experience as they realize universal concepts of personal and professional development from the Older and Younger Facilitators. As you read, you will notice a word or phrase printed in italics with a small number following in superscript; these are your models, methods and tools, which are described in more detail in Part Two. As you read the story, if something is of particular interest, you can go to Part Two and read a description of it. The number indicates the order in which the tool is listed in Part Two. This platform creates a process allowing you to discover how you can apply these principles to your individual situation. Ultimately, this story is about you.

We encourage you to begin listing your new discoveries, as well as those you may already be aware of that are not listed in this book.

A third resource is our website, **www.SeekingTrueNorth.com,** which presents excerpts from this book, more details on tools and examples of how others are seeking and living True North.

PART I
The Story of Freedom
and Beautiful

Prelude

Freedom

As you begin reading this book, you should know a few things about our main character, Freedom. To give you a better understanding of him, we must first step back in time.

Freedom felt unfulfilled in his life. At home, he had a lovely wife and two wonderful children. He felt his marriage was fine, yet deep down he knew that there were ways to make it better.

In the last six months, Freedom had been downsized by his previous employer and had transitioned to a position as financial officer in a different company. He struggled to perform in his new role of leading and inspiring his team of employees. Freedom attempted to use many strategies that he had learned over the years, yet often they did not work as effectively as he would have liked. As a result, a certain amount of resentment and sarcasm had seeped into his thinking and communication.

Now he felt a longing inside for something more meaningful and fulfilling.

Beautiful

Beautiful is the name of the lead female character of our story. We think you will appreciate and respect her.

Beautiful longs for a fresh sense of love and vitality in her life. At home, she is happy being a mother to her only child. Unfortunately, she does not have the same fulfillment in her relationship with her husband. Beautiful struggles with a lack of self-confidence. Her lack of self-worth ignites a cry deep within her to be admired as a beautiful person.

Beautiful does well in her managerial role at work; yet, despite her many faithfully performed responsibilities, she receives little reward or recognition.

Being strong and determined, she wants regeneration and refreshment and will not quit until she finds it.

With these thoughts in mind, let's begin the story.

Prepare

Once upon a time, in a land not so very far away from here, lived a man named Freedom. What Freedom wanted most in life was to be happy. He wanted to enjoy his work and his relationships with family and friends. He wanted to feel free and be free.

Freedom was on a mission to find the happiness and satisfaction he desired. He had read many books and listened to many tapes on self-improvement, business and leadership. He had learned about more than the seven habits of successful people; he knew a few financial, business and personal success strategies, and he practiced some positive thinking. He had been to many seminars, retreats and conferences. But Freedom was not content. Frankly, he was tired of all the gurus' success formulas. He simply wished he could have the freedom and happiness he desired, at both work and home.

Freedom sighed and said, "Here I go again." It was the opening of a four-day leadership retreat for an association he belonged to. He had been to retreats before and usually became bored within the first 15 minutes. He hoped that this time, he would have some sort of breakthrough to take him to the next level in his quest — without being bored to death in the process.

Freedom was skeptical. Once he met several of the other people attending the retreat, he found that he was not alone. It seemed to Freedom that many of the so-called "gurus" he had encountered had lots of strategies and advice, but few had the simple, practical tools necessary to attain what they deemed as success.

So here he was, at the opening evening of yet another retreat. There were two facilitators, one older and one younger. Freedom listened to the Younger Facilitator welcome the participants. Standing erect with his arms and hands at his side and his feet shoulder-width apart, the Younger Facilitator confidently announced, "Over the next four days, we will all be climbing mountains. Don't worry: We won't literally be climbing, but we will be ascending a mountain of mastery in our own lives." He drew a picture of three mountains on the flip chart.

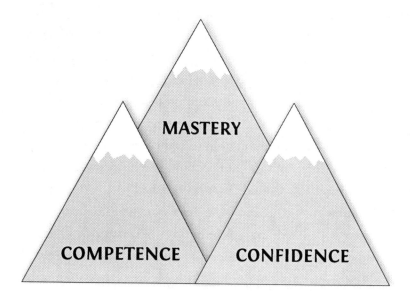

"The big mountain in the back is called *Mastery Mountain*[1]. The two smaller mountains in the front are Competence Mountain and Confidence Mountain. In everything we learn, we climb these mountains over and over again. You will learn about the many features of these mountains in the days ahead. As you consider your approach to Mastery Mountain, your first challenge is to decide whether you are a *Prisoner, Vacationer or Leader*[2]."

Freedom snapped out of his own thinking and looked at the
words on the flip chart as he tried to listen.

Leader

Vacationer

Prisoner

"You came here as one of the three," explained the Younger
Facilitator. "Perhaps you came as a Prisoner because someone
told you that you had to be here. Maybe you came as a Vacationer
because at worst you will get time off from work in a nice place. You
may have come as a Leader, prepared for a positive, life-changing
experience. The same is true in all we think and do. If you desire to be
better in sales, better in leadership, better in your role as a manager or
better in your relationships, preparation is essential. This attitude tool
is a must in your growth and development.

"Each moment of each and every day, you live your life as a
Prisoner, a Vacationer, or a Leader. The choice is yours to make.
Regardless of which you are now, our expectation is that you will
decide to be leaders and to help others to do the same.

"We intend to provide you, as leaders of others, with many
models, methods, tools and habits designed to assist in leading
yourself and others toward more fulfilling and meaningful lives."

The Younger Facilitator then drew a picture of a compass on the
flip chart.

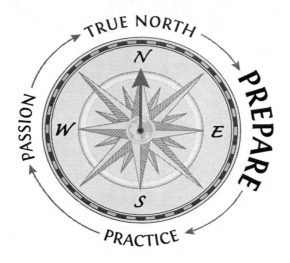

"This is called the True North Compass. It provides direction for systematically using the models, methods and tools along the pathway to achieving desired results. The True North Compass is composed of four major parts. Today, we will be introducing these four components and reinforcing the concepts throughout our time together. The first part of the True North Compass model is called Prepare.'

"If we are to live effective, meaningful lives," the Younger Facilitator continued, "then we must prepare. Likewise a successful retreat begins with preparation.

"Have you prepared yourself to have a successful retreat? Right now, at the very beginning, I will add that you may want to consider this 'retreat' as an *'Advance*[3].' This experience represents an opportunity to advance in many aspects of your daily lives; our choices of words and thoughts are very influential.

"Consider these words of wisdom: *'When the student is ready, the teacher appears*[4].' So, have you prepared for this experience? Over the next four days, if you are prepared, you may be surprised to meet with new ' teachers' in unique ways. If you are not prepared, you may not even notice the teachers when they appear, or you may say to yourself, 'I don't need that teacher now.'

"Teachers appear in many forms, just as God speaks in many ways. We must continually prepare our minds, bodies and spirits to be in the most receptive state for positive growth. We tend to select information supporting the belief systems that we already have in place about the world. And we all have spent a lot of time *forming judgments and assumptions*[5] that cause us to miss our 'teachers.' Where and when in your life are you missing your teachers, and why? Where and when are you not seeing, hearing or sensing potential breakthroughs or serendipitous messages?"

Freedom's attention was broken like a record scratch. "Did he just say, 'just as God speaks'? Oh great," thought Freedom. "He's talking about God! I didn't know this was going to be a religious thing." Then Freedom said to himself, sarcastically, "Next thing he'll say is, 'Your mind is like a parachute. It works best when it's open.'" Freedom's skepticism was getting the best of him.

The Younger Facilitator looked slowly around the room, *making eye contact*[6] with many of the participants as he spoke. "Many of us have heard the phrase, 'Luck is when preparedness meets opportunity.' Are you prepared to meet opportunity? To be prepared in this way, you must choose what you want to be prepared for, and determine your desired end results.

"You do this by asking yourself the value-based *Most Important Question*[7]: 'What is most important to me in my _____?' Fill in the blank with your focus area, such as life, business or relationships.

"As this concept relates to our upcoming time together, your first assignment is to complete this sentence, known as the *Magic Statement*[8]: 'This was the best workshop experience I have ever had because_____.'

"First, visualize yourself returning home at the conclusion of this retreat. Imagine that someone close to you comes up and asks, 'So, how was your retreat?' You reply by saying, 'The retreat was the best workshop experience I have ever had because [blank],' and you fill in the rest," explained the Younger Facilitator. "Write out the ending of this statement as if the four-day workshop were over and you were home explaining the experience to a family member, fellow employee or friend. Visualize how the experience *looks, sounds and feels*[9] as you write."

Freedom looked around at the other participants and thought, "I wonder what they will write." He found it difficult to imagine the workshop already being over.

After a few minutes, the Younger Facilitator asked if anyone would be willing to share what he or she had written. "And please, *give your name*[10] before you read," he added.

"Oh great," thought Freedom, "We all have to share our answers."

The 24 people sat comfortably in a circle and, one by one, read their statements aloud.

Freedom read his statement:

My name is Freedom. This was the best workshop experience I have ever had because I've been to these things before, and I hoped that this time I would get some tools that would help me be a better leader in my job and for our association — and I did.

"I could have said a lot more," thought Freedom as he finished reading his statement to the group, "but if I get even half of what I have visualized in my magic statement out of this, it will have been worth it."

Partway around the room, directly across from Freedom, a woman spoke. "My name is Beautiful," she said, "and this is what I wrote."

This was the best workshop experience I have ever had because I came away with some different ways to be happier and more effective in my life, work and relationships. Also, I was inspired and equipped to feel and know that I am a beautiful person sharing the wealth of life with others.

"Oh my gosh," Beautiful thought to herself. "I hope that sounded okay."

Freedom stared in wonder at the woman as she spoke. She seemed confident, pleasant and sincere. "I must find out more about her," he thought.

The Younger Facilitator spoke after all had read. "Thank you, everyone. Now we have heard what each of us hopes to achieve from our four days together. Remember, this preparation tool is one that can be used at the outset of any experience. Visualizing and articulating our desired end results allow us to not just live our future, but to create it. I also want you to consider what we did *not* hear from each other. One thing we did not hear about is the reason behind our desired end results. This is the *'why' tool*[11].

"Each of us brings a unique history to this conference. We all have reasons for seeking what we seek. Having a strong, compelling reason for the things that we want to achieve gives us an amazing power to create the 'how.' Consider that clarity of your purpose is equally as important as achieving the results you desire.

"I want you to keep your statement with you at all times and *recite it to yourself often*[12]. Share it with your fellow participants here, and talk about it. Most of all, be prepared for your" — here the Younger Facilitator held up his fingers in quotation marks as he spoke — "quote, 'teachers,' to appear and guide you, providing you with the tools necessary to bring your desired results to fruition."

The Younger Facilitator glanced slowly around the room, making eye contact with each person, and then spoke again. "You are here for only four days of your precious life. We encourage you to take these four days seriously.

"You have begun the process by writing and sharing your desired end results. We have given each of you a notebook in which to keep a *personal journal*[13], and we want you to use it effectively. It is important to write out your clearly defined desired end results, together with the date by which you will achieve them. This step will help you in all of your preparation for effective living.

"Now, we want you to continue writing about preparing yourself for a life-enhancing experience here over the next four days. The value of recording your experiences in your journal won't be in remembering what we say, but rather in remembering and *writing what you think*[14] in response to what we say.

"We challenge you to write down your thoughts and ideas; to begin this process, we ask you to write down more than *100 goals*[15] you would like to achieve in your life. Be sure to include the date by which you plan to achieve each one. You can refer back to this journal often to measure your growth and success.

"We want you to practice the tools you receive while you are here. The first habit we want you to practice is to Prepare. You have chosen to be prepared for a positive experience here. You have chosen what you want to be prepared for and have written out your clearly defined desired end results. Now you must confidently expect to achieve these results — results full of purpose and meaning — four days hence.

"Expect that you will achieve those results; do not merely 'hope' to achieve them. Often, if we settle for merely 'hoping' for a result, what we are really doing is entertaining the possibility of *not* achieving our goal.

"To *expect* is to be confident in our beliefs and actions to achieve what we set out to do. This is called 'being prepared.'"

The facilitator then turned over a new flip chart sheet, which read:

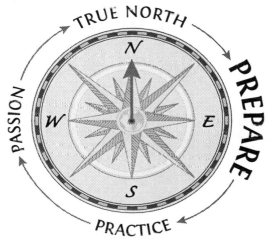

It Is Very Simple to Prepare:

1. Choose what you want to be prepared for...

...and determine your desired end results.

2. Write out your clearly defined desired end results...

...including a date by which you will achieve them.

3. Expect that you will achieve your desired end results...

...results full of purpose and meaning.

Practice

The Older Facilitator now rose, standing with confidence, just as the Younger Facilitator had when he had begun speaking. As the Older Facilitator slowly gazed around the room, he made eye contact and smiled at each person. Then he began to speak.

"We have heard from our Younger Facilitator about the importance of being prepared. By the way, let's give him a nice *round of applause*[16]. Isn't he incredible! *Take your finger and point*[17] with me at our Younger Facilitator. Now repeat after me, with enthusiasm, 'You are incredible!'" As the entire group simultaneously and enthusiastically pointed and repeated the chant, laughter broke out from everyone in the room.

"Now take your finger, *poke yourself*[18] in the chest, and repeat after me, 'You know what? I am incredible too!'" Again, the laughter burst out.

Freedom was having fun. He looked across the room and smiled at Beautiful, who returned the same to him.

The Older Facilitator continued, "Now that is called 'Practice.' We just practiced bringing about what you wrote about being prepared for — namely, that you expect positive experiences here. Our next group challenge provides a way to heighten our awareness of positive experiences."

The Older Facilitator then led the group in a fun interactive challenge called the *Story of the Right Advance*[19], in which the participants were assigned a secret person to observe and instructed to catch people doing "right" throughout the retreat. "***The gift***[20] you brought with you will be given to your secret person on the last day of our time together," added the Older Facilitator. "At that time, you will summarize the many positives you have observed over the four days. This part of the True North Compass model is called 'Practice'." He wrote the word on the flip chart.

"The first component of practice is to seek out the model, method or tool you desire to utilize," the Older Facilitator continued. "I am proud to say that I am a third-generation carpenter. Now, a carpenter needs many tools and skills to build the beautiful homes, cabinets and furniture he creates. Just like the carpenter, we, as leaders, need tools and skills to lead others and ourselves. And, just like a carpenter, when we acquire a new tool, we must practice using it safely and effectively. In our quest to find meaning, fulfillment and purpose in our lives, we must seek for and use the right tools at the right times.

"When learning a new technique, we must first choose the right tool or skill, the one that will most effectively assist us. Remember that success leaves clues. By seeking out those who have achieved the results we are after, we can discover the methods that those people used most successfully to reach their own goals. Just like the time-tested apprenticeship system, we all need to find masters in our field of study. The masters will lead us to the correct use of the tools we select. Our masters, or mentors, may come from many sources, including the books we read, the people we meet and those whom we specifically search out. These **mentors**[21] become our coaches in the process of becoming mentors ourselves. After seeking out our mentors, obtaining advice and gathering information, we carefully select our new tools and skills. Next, we must commit ourselves to practicing with these new tools and skills until they become ingrained into our beings.

"The ancient Greek philosopher Aristotle once said, 'We are what we repeatedly do. Excellence, then, is not an act, but a habit.' It takes much consistent practice for the use of a new skill or tool to become a habit in our lives. Then to really lock it in, we must begin to teach this new skill or tool to others, thus becoming mentors ourselves. Remember, a tool is made to be used. The **highest order of learning**[22] is when a concept is passed on to another person, who can then pass that on to someone else."

The Older Facilitator wrote a formula on the flip chart, smiling and lifting one eyebrow as he did so. "As we examine all the models, methods and tools that we must practice," he said, "consider the following equation:

$$\textbf{\textit{Values + Beliefs + Actions =}}$$
$$\textbf{\textit{State of Mind or Being}}$$

"Values plus beliefs plus your actions equal a state of mind or being," he said aloud, paraphrasing the formula. "Let's start by examining the foundation of this equation that guides our decisions. Every one of us human beings has a set of *core values*[23] that guides us in making decisions about everything in our lives. Both consciously and subconsciously, we filter information through our core values to decide what to do. 'Values' can be defined as standards or rules that provide guidance for living out what is most important in life. These values can be bad, good or a combination thereof.

"In your journal, I want each of you to list at least 10 core values that guide you in your life. List those that you currently live out every day: virtuous and benevolent values like security, adventure, family and commitment; and destructive and malevolent values, such as laziness, lying, cheating and stealing. Take a look in the mirror and be honest with yourself."

The Older Facilitator then walked up to Freedom, poked him in the shoulder and laughingly said, "If you have lying on your values list, you might want to consider deleting that." Everyone laughed. "Face yourself squarely and write down who you really are. Remember that the past does not equal the future. Despite our weaknesses and failures, we have the choice to create a better today and tomorrow."

After a few minutes' silence so that his audience could think and write, the Older Facilitator resumed speaking. "Now think through the core values on your list and decide what you would like to add to or delete from your life. Your goal here is to set up an ideal list of values for how you want to live your life."

Freedom thought, "I wonder how my values and beliefs need to be realigned."

"Another way to look at this," continued the Older Facilitator, "is to create your own self-fulfilling prophecy, sometimes known as the *Pygmalion Effect*[24] — creating expectations of positive decisions you will make. Then revise your list and put your values in order of priority.

"We want you to review your values every morning while you are here and when you return home. You may also want to consider how your values compare to those held by people with whom you have a significant relationship. When we make decisions with another person, it is critical to understand why we want to make certain decisions.

"One way to reinforce your values is to create a ***personal motto***[25]. This statement reminds you of who you want to be and how you want to live your life. Incorporate your values into this short statement to keep you on track every day.

"Now let's consider the second part of this equation — beliefs."

The Younger Facilitator interjected, "If you can believe it, you can achieve it! Hallelujah!"

The Older Facilitator paused, stared at the Younger Facilitator, and with both eyebrows raised, said, "Thanks for that positive interruption and vote of confidence." Everyone laughed again.

"As I was saying," he went on, "beliefs can be defined as convictions or faith to live out our values. Remember that values plus beliefs plus your actions equal a state of mind or being. Our belief systems directly impact the quality and quantity of action that we take. When we take action, our state of mind is directly related to how aligned our actions are with those values and beliefs. Values and beliefs are a means to the actions we strive to take in life. The end, ultimately, is always a state of mind or being." The Older Facilitator wrote the following summary questions on the flip chart:

What state of being are you seeking?

What values guide your decisions?

What beliefs must you have?

What actions must you take?

Then he added, "These choices will determine your state of mind or being." The group pondered the Older Facilitator's questions.

Over the next several hours, the Younger and Older Facilitators led the group in a variety of activities. One involved role-playing to explore the differences among the **Commander, Partner and Facilitator Leadership Styles**[26]; in another, the participants joined in **setting group values**[27] for their four days together.

The list of group values was written on the flip chart and taped on the wall. "Fun" was high on the list. Other suggestions, such as "Building Trust," "Respect," "Openness to Creativity" and "Return on Investment" were discussed and agreed to through the **thumb-check assessment**[28] tool.

The Younger Facilitator reviewed the **Emotional Intelligence Assessment**[29] that participants had taken prior to arriving. This included an **interactive card game**[30], in which the 15 competencies were reviewed and discussed. "Your EQ Assessment is a valuable tool for your growth and development," he said. "One powerful way to begin developing these competencies is through the use of positive **affirmations**[31]. Positive affirmations work when you believe and tell yourself to *act-as-if.* This is another tool to help us create who we want to be and how we want to act."

"Remember," the Older Facilitator added, "when creating affirmations, write them in the active, present tense, in a positive mode. And, to be effective, your affirmations must be aligned with your core values and beliefs."

The Younger Facilitator then went on to **divide the group into four quadrants**[32], according to the season in which they were born. "All of you who were born in summer, move to this section of the room."

The Older Facilitator then asked the group to discuss their expectations. At one point, the Older Facilitator joined the small group in which Freedom, Beautiful and four others were engaged in a lively discussion.

"Do you think your expectations will be met here over the next four days?" the facilitator interjected.

Freedom spoke up and said, "I think it is possible."

"How do you mean, Freedom?" prompted the Older Facilitator.

Freedom, surprised to hear the Older Facilitator call him by name, answered thoughtfully, "Well, I think if we really put forth an effort, we should be able to have at least some of our expectations met."

"How do we know what all your expectations are?" the Older Facilitator asked.

"I would have to speak up and tell you what my expectations are," Freedom replied.

"That's right," said the Older Facilitator, and turning to the next page on the flip chart, he drew the *Expectations Quadrant Model*[33].

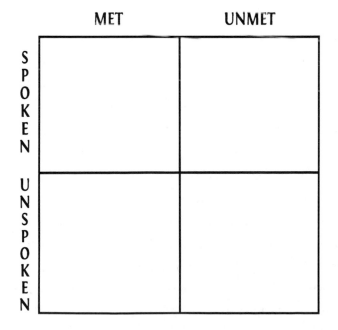

"By communicating expectations, we are moving from unspoken to spoken in the managing expectations quadrant. Often, the biggest cause of frustration when working in a team stems from unspoken and unmet expectations."

One by one, calling each by name, the Older Facilitator asked the group members individually the same question he had asked generally before: "Do you think your expectations will be met here over the next four days?" Freedom was astonished that he knew all their names. "How do you *memorize names*[34] so quickly?" he wondered.

At one point, the group was getting pretty rowdy, and the Older Facilitator taught them how to quiet a group quickly by using the *Hand of Reason*[35].

After each person shared an answer to his question, the Older Facilitator followed up with another question: "*How do you mean?*[36]"

"I'd really like to work on expressing my feelings better," Freedom thought as he listened to the other group members. "And I wish I felt more confident about speaking up when I have an idea I believe would be helpful. So many times, I keep silent only to regret it later." As he thought over the many challenges in his own life and his lack of assertiveness, he knew he wanted to improve in these areas. He began to wonder what this "Seeking True North " stuff was all about.

Suddenly, the Younger Facilitator blew a wooden whistle that sounded just like a *train whistle*[37]. When the room fell silent, the Older Facilitator spoke up. "We want you to form a *continuum*[38] based on your level of confidence as a leader in your workplace. Please form a continuous line in single file and place yourself somewhere in the line. Those of you who feel very confident as leaders in your workplace, move toward this end of the room. And, those of you who feel the least sure of yourselves as leaders in your workplace, move toward that end of the room. Complete this exercise without any verbal communication."

Freedom thought, "Well, I think I'm a good leader, but I am not as sure of myself as I want to be. I don't speak up as much as I should. But I don't want others to think I am a loser, so I'd better go down near the confident leaders. Let's see where the others place themselves, and I will plug myself in then." He settled for a place near the middle, a few places toward the more experienced, confident end of the continuum, noticing as he did so that Beautiful was almost exactly opposite in the continuum to his own position.

They were now instructed to break into small groups again and share with each other why they chose to be where they were in the continuum. Throughout the activity, the Older and the Younger Facilitators continued to *wander around and connect*[39] with each person, smiling, nodding and affirming as they listened.

After a few minutes of discussion, the Younger Facilitator blew the train whistle and asked, "Who can tell me what a **Ready Circle**[40] is?"

Beautiful spoke up. "A Ready Circle is a circle in which you can see the eyes of every other person in the circle."

"That's very good, Beautiful. Now if you would all please form a Ready Circle."

Once in the circle, the Older Facilitator asked, "So, what have we been doing over the past few hours?"

Again, Beautiful answered. "Preparing and practicing," she said, with a big smile on her face.

"Exactly," said the Older Facilitator.

Freedom thought, "Gee, my first answer was 'having fun.'"

As if he had read Freedom's mind, the Older Facilitator asked, "Did you have fun practicing?"

They all replied with a hearty "Yes!"

"We must keep practicing until our new tool or skill becomes an 'Unconscious Competence,'" the Older Facilitator replied. "We reach a level of unconscious competence when we are so good at something that we can actively 'do' it without even thinking about it. And now I want to explain to you one model that helps us understand the process of change and growth. In this model, which we call the **Zoning-In Model**[41], there are three zones. We tend to stay in the 'familiar' zone because we hold on to what we know and do often. Some call it the 'comfort' zone. Next is the 'growth' zone. This is where we must force ourselves to practice our chosen new tools and skills." He drew the model on the flipchart.

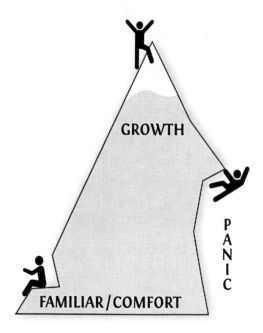

"And third is the 'panic' zone, where we find ourselves scared because we don't know what we are doing. Do these zones sound familiar to any of you?"

Many people chuckled and responded with "Yes."

"I encourage you as leaders and as people who choose to create a positive future to force yourselves into the growth zone over and over and over again, until it becomes familiar. Now, why is it that most people have difficulty going into the growth zone?"

"Fear of failure," suggested one of the participants.

"Very good," said the Older Facilitator. "History tells us that many of the greatest leaders have also failed the most. Deep inside, each of us knows that failure is a natural part of growth in life. Failure is nothing more than not yet producing the results you desire."

The Older Facilitator then led the participants in discussing the process of managing change and entering the growth zone.

"There is usually some frustration — even pain — attached to the growth process," the Older Facilitator reminded them. "Yet, this is where the life-enhancing experiences occur and the breakthroughs happen. You must force yourself into the growth zone and take consistent action. This is where you create a leadership life that is truly fulfilling. I challenge you to commit to forcing yourself into the growth zone and *practice for 12 months*[42]."

"A most important part of practicing in the growth zone is developing what we call *sensory acuity*[43]. Seek feedback and focus on the process as you adapt your strategy to achieve your desired end results. This involves paying specific attention to what is working and what is not. As you practice, make sure you are consciously monitoring your progress as you challenge your personal limits and embrace your growth zone. *Seek the opinions of others*[44] about how they perceive your growth. Do it! Test it out for yourself. It's the only way you will know if it brings about incredible growth in your life. By continuously paying attention to what is working, you can actively adapt your strategy to achieve the results you desire. As you continue the process, remember that the powerful 'why' will keep you on track. When you continually focus on how to live in your growth zone, I guarantee you will be happier, feel more confident as a leader, live more profitably, look better, feel better and have healthier relationships in your life."

As he listened, Freedom felt a new sense of energy and determination. "I really want this," he thought. "I desire to have a life filled with more positive meaning and purpose. I am going to grow in the next 12 months." He looked over at Beautiful. She seemed to be deep in thought as she stared out the window at the mountains.

After a time, the Older Facilitator called for everyone's attention. "Please sit down and relax," he said, smiling. "It's time to introduce another tool, *storytelling*[45]. I want to close this session by telling you a story:

"A little over a hundred years ago, there lived a young orphan girl. She and her brother, both sickly, were moved to an orphanage. Shortly after that, her brother became ill and died.

The girl became so sad and despondent that she gave up living. She curled up in a fetal position and just did not respond to anyone.

"At that period in history and in that orphanage, people in her condition were simply put in a cell and left alone. Curled up in her cell, the girl did not eat, speak or respond. She was dying.

"Now in that orphanage was a woman who was responsible for cleaning the facility. She was the mop woman. She was also responsible for caring for the untreated 'patients' in the cells. After many days of attempting to talk to the girl in the cell, the mop woman took the handle of her mop and began to poke at the girl lying on the floor. The mop woman poked and goaded the girl until the girl began to make guttural noises and tried to hit the mop handle away.

"No longer left to die peacefully, forced to respond to the goading of the mop woman, the girl began to eat. In time, she became healthy again.

"Later in her life, she became Helen Keller's teacher."

"Can any of you tell me who she was?" asked the Older Facilitator.

"Anne Sullivan," replied one of the participants.

"That's right. But most people don't know about the mop woman. Goading or challenging someone else is similar to the one-minute reprimand, where you correct or guide someone else. However, you must be open to being instructed or guided by someone else as well. I challenge you to become a 'Mop Woman,'" the Older Facilitator said in a soft, firm voice filled with deep conviction. "I challenge you to become a person who goads and pokes others to become better in their lives. But you must remember that you can never rightfully goad someone else unless you yourself are willing to be goaded."

There was silence in the room.

Freedom pondered the Older Facilitator's challenge.

The next few seconds seemed like minutes. The Older Facilitator broke the silence and again spoke in a soft voice. "Reach over to your neighbor on your right and poke him or her in the shoulder. Then repeat after me, 'You know what?'"

Every person responded, poking his and her neighbor while saying in a soft voice, "You know what?"

"I'm glad you're here," the Older Facilitator continued while poking Freedom, who happened to be sitting on his right.

The entire group, continuing to poke their neighbors, whispered with smiling faces, "I'm glad you're here."

It Is Very Simple to Practice

1. **Seek out and choose...**

   ... the Model, Method or Tool you desire to utilize.

2. **Force yourself into the Growth Zone...**

   ... and take consistent action.

3. **Seek feedback and focus on the process...**

   ... as you adapt your strategy to achieve desired end results.

Passion

After moving the group outside on the lawn and gathering in a Ready Circle, the Younger Facilitator blew his train whistle and gathered the attention of the group. Then the Older Facilitator spoke. "Several years ago, I went rock climbing with the Younger Facilitator, who was to coach me in the art of technical climbing. I was very excited. As we walked along the trail toward the rocks, I wanted to chat about the birds, great weather and beautiful views. But I looked over at the Younger Facilitator to see him walking fast and staring straight ahead at the trail. He slapped his hands together, rubbed them and began to breathe deep breaths as we kept up the fast pace. I started to say something about going too fast, but then I realized what he was doing. He was preparing for the climb. Well, I got a little scared. Then I thought I'd better practice what I preach, so I started to match his pace, his hand-slapping, and his intense focus on the climbing ahead. I wasn't sure what to focus on, but I knew that the Younger Facilitator, a world-class rock climber, did know. He was clearly focused, intense, envisioning the climb, rehearsing and practicing, all in his mind, before we ever arrived at the rocks."

Just then, Freedom spoke up. "I can visualize the scene on the way to the rock climb, but what is the hand-slapping all about?"

"Great question," the Older Facilitator responded. "By slapping his hands together, the Younger Facilitator was firing off what we call an *anchor*. This was his way to prepare for the climb by getting his body and mind into a peak state. This principle of *psychological anchors and triggers*[46] is one of the most powerful concepts I have ever come across. Let me explain.

"How many of you have been driving down the road when you heard a song that reminded you of an amazing, positive experience you had with a friend? You heard the song and cranked up the volume. The next thing you knew, your body was tingling and you had a big smile on your face because you were reliving the experience. I am sure that is something we can all relate to. So why does that happen? What was the song?"

Beautiful replied, "A trigger."

"That's right, Beautiful, a *trigger* — a portal that connects your past and present through emotional and chemical connections. That trigger is what we refer to as an anchor. Question: How did that trigger come about?"

"Well," Beautiful jumped in, "we created an association to that song when we had an experience or were with that person, and when we heard the song later, the same feelings we had in the initial experience came back."

"Exactly," the Older Facilitator agreed. "In that particular moment, that anchor is determining our emotional state. So, let me ask you this: How many anchors and triggers, along with the emotional states that they elicit, do you think you could list? There are lots when we begin to think about them. Even more fascinating are the subconscious triggers that have an impact on us that we aren't even aware of. To bring this around full circle, the Younger Facilitator had created an anchor to support the process of getting into a positive, powerful state before starting a difficult climb."

"Did you say *created* the anchor? What do you mean?" asked Freedom.

"Well, Freedom, creating an anchor is creating a powerful association to a specific word, phrase or action. In this instance, the

Younger Facilitator created an association linking total confidence and power to the slapping of his hands."

"How?" Freedom asked. "How do you do that?"

"You can do this by reflecting on powerful emotional states that you have experienced in your past, and then associating them to something you do in the present. You see, the thing is, we already do it all the time. The question is, how can we be purposeful about it?

"Now tell me: How does the concept of anchors relate to passion?"

"Well," Freedom responded, "it sounds as if anchors are a way that you can create passion at any moment you want!"

"Exactly. We all have the ability to control our emotional states. At any given moment, you have the power to move from being stressed to being calm and relaxed, or from being nervous to being totally confident. The more we understand about anchors, the more we will be able to control our states of being in body, mind and spirit."

Then the Older Facilitator continued his story.

"As I was saying about the rock climbing experience, I knew this man to be passionate about rock climbing. I thought, 'I am glad to be here with him.'" Turning toward the Younger Facilitator, he added, "I also realize that he is passionate about being a leader who influences others to do great things. Again, I am glad to be with him." As the Younger Facilitator smiled, the Older Facilitator gave him a big bear hug. They slapped high fives and laughed. Turning toward the participants again, the Older Facilitator said, "Letting someone know what you honestly admire in him or her is important; to *edify another*[47] is a great tool for making a positive difference in that person's life. With that said, I want you to give your attention to our Younger Facilitator as he shares the next step in the pathway to Seeking True North."

The Younger Facilitator turned and looked at each person in the Ready Circle and said, "The next part of the True North Compass is called 'Passion.'"

He pointed to some distant mountains and said, "Developing passion is kind of like hiking up those four mountains we see in the distance. We call this next model the *Passion Mountain Model*[48]." He then scratched in the dirt an outline of the four mountains.

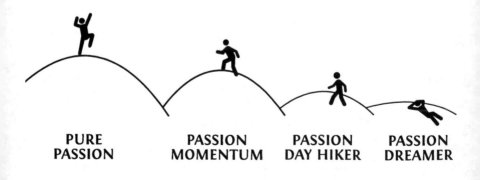

| PURE PASSION | PASSION MOMENTUM | PASSION DAY HIKER | PASSION DREAMER |

"On this lowest mountain, which we call Passion Dreamer Mountain, is a person lying back, just dreaming about something he would love to do. And that is a very good thing. However, many people spend their entire lives here in their familiar zone and never force themselves into the growth zone to bring about the desired end results they dream about. On the next higher mountain, which we call Passion Day Hike Mountain, is a person who does a little trek, stirring up some interest and passion toward achieving a specific goal. In the pursuit of our interests, we will all find ourselves on this mountain at times as we explore the possibilities. This mountain is where you make a conscious decision to create happiness and meaning in your life."

He continued drawing his sketches in the dirt. "The next higher mountain is called Passion Momentum Mountain. Here, an individual is moving positively toward bringing desired end results to fruition. The climb may be steep and difficult at times, but persistence, determination and a stalwart attitude make all the difference. You will be in the growth zone a lot here. The fourth and highest summit is called Pure Passion Mountain. This is where you are just in the flow of movement, in the power of the now, enjoying all the challenges and accomplishments, and are already in gear for the next desired outcome. But be warned: there is a potential trap here. Some people stay on one of these mountains and never progress to the attainment of their desired results."

Over the next hour, the Younger Facilitator led the group in several valuable, thought-provoking, interactive challenges. One, called the **Pathway**[49], seemed to be a favorite with all. It explored emotional milestones in each person's history as a means of determining energy and focus for the future. After each challenge, the participants took a few minutes to engage in **reflection**[50] about the initiative and discuss its relevance to their lives, work, leadership responsibilities, and of course, "Passion."

It was during one of these debrief sessions that Freedom spoke up. "These are great initiatives we are learning and participating in. I plan to use some of them back home with my teams, but how do we make passion an everyday habit in our lives?"

"I was just thinking the same thing," Beautiful added eagerly. "How do we?" Many heads nodded in agreement, and they all turned to the Younger Facilitator to await his response.

"I have no idea," he answered, and he shook his head as if in bewilderment. "I was hoping you might be able to tell *me* that."

There was silence.

The Younger Facilitator waited a few moments, and then smiled. "Just kidding," he said. "Actually, I am on a quest in life, just like you, to find the answer to this question. However, I have spent a great deal of time processing what passion seems to mean and how I can have it on a continuous basis in my life. So, in essence, the *first* step to creating passion is to focus on what it means to you and how you can create it. Remember, you get what you focus on.

"The first key insight is that the foundation for passion comes from being fully present in *this* moment. We refer to this as **embracing the now**[51]. Many people spend their lives focused on the past or consumed with concern over the future. How much of your time is spent reflecting on the past and thinking about the future? When we realize that passion is a state that occurs in the present, we can begin to experience life more fully. You see, the biggest challenge is to control our minds, so that we can allow ourselves to fully experience the present moment; embracing the 'now' is a choice we all can make.

"Am I saying that we shouldn't focus on the future to create the life that we want to live? Of course not, but passion comes only in the present moment. If you want more of it, decide to be fully engaged in the now, more of the time.

"Here are a few other concepts that I have found critical to creating passion in our lives. The first is one I refer to as the **Prax Factor**[52]. The Prax Factor means that the quality of our lives is directly related to the people we choose to surround ourselves with. Associating with people who have negative attitudes and limiting beliefs about what you can do does not further your goals and dreams. Be very careful when choosing the people you spend time with. We must surround ourselves with a supportive team of friends who encourage us toward our full potential. And continually seek out those people who have the characteristics and qualities that you want in your life. Soon enough, those qualities will be integrated into your system, helping you to live the life that is most important to you. If more passion in your life is what you seek, surround yourself with passionate people.

"The next concept relates to how we respond to situations. Remember that passion is a choice. In every moment, we have the ability to choose our attitudes and responses to any given situation. You can look at something one way and be sad and depressed. You can also **reframe the meaning**[53] of that experience and seek out the positive possibilities. If your first response to an experience is negative, stop. Consider an alternative viewpoint. Make this a continuous habit, until processing the positive possibilities is your norm. Good friends often help us do this.

"Let me give you a practical example of how I prepare, practice and create passion. Recently, I planned a trip to Thailand to explore business opportunities for corporate retreats and to climb some of the most beautiful rock on the planet. How did I create passion for this short-term venture? In creating passion, you must feed your body, mind and spirit positive healthy food and embrace the process with every step in your pathway.

"I chose to get passionate about making this trip one of the most incredibly awesome and valuable experiences I have ever had. I began to 'Prepare' in several ways. In my *'I Envision' Booklet*[54] I began to write out the details of desired end results from this experience. All the dates were carefully scheduled. Realizing what it would take to climb at the level I desired, I orchestrated an intensive 10-week physical *conditioning program*[55]. Things like core strength training, swimming and climbing-specific workouts with expert climbers laid the foundation. I also focused on *nutrition*[56] and *hydration*[57]. And by the way, balanced nutrition, adequate hydration and a certain amount of daily physical conditioning are vital to a healthy life filled with passion and effectiveness.

"Then, for the mental 'Practice,' which ties in with the 'Passion,' ' I specifically wrote out positive affirmation statements and beliefs about the experience before it ever happened. Many of them revolved around being fully present and focusing on heightened awareness of each experience that I was to come across. Next, I used *mental imaging*[58] to visualize the specific types of climbs I would participate in. Also, before I ever arrived, I created a *Virtual Reality Vision Board*[59] with photos and pictorial details of climbing at various locations in Thailand."

"Excuse me," interjected Freedom. "What is a Virtual Reality Vision Board?"

"Good question, Freedom," responded the Younger Facilitator. "It is simply a poster board with a collage of pictures, words, magazine photos, and so on of all you want to accomplish. But you must insert photos of yourself into the other pictures on the vision board. You are projecting future events on this board — seeing yourself already accomplishing what you want to achieve. You are forecasting your images, thoughts and words on a vision board before they ever happen. It is a powerful tool."

"I think I understand what you are saying," Freedom responded, "but will that system work for making your life happier and your relationships and work more rewarding?"

"What do the rest of you think?" asked the Younger Facilitator. Several people shared their thoughts, and then Beautiful spoke up. "If I apply the same system to my desired end results for this workshop, it could sound something like this:

"First, I *prepare* by choosing to become happier, have better relationships and enjoy my work more. Second, I choose a few tools to *practice* with. I choose to create positive affirmations and beliefs about being happier at work and in my relationships. I also choose the tool of writing out 100 specific goals about how it will look, sound and feel to be happier in my work and relationships. And third, I choose the tool of the Virtual Reality Vision Board and create a collage of my work and relationship lives being happier and more effective.

"So I just did what you did for your Thailand experience, only I plugged in my own desired end results. Did I do it right?"

"Indeed, you did," the Younger Facilitator responded. "You prepare by creating your vision, and practice by choosing and using tools to help you achieve that vision. And let's not forget: When is the only time that passion can take place?"

Beautiful responded, "Right now."

"Yes, right now. Let's give this beautiful woman a round of applause," said the Younger Facilitator with a smile on his face. Everyone looked at Beautiful and applauded. Beautiful felt a flood of positive emotions as she recognized her confidence level growing.

"Who is this woman?" Freedom thought to himself. "She just grabbed the whole concept and blurted it out like she is already using it!" Then he spoke aloud.

"That is all great," he said. "But what do you do when something happens that is dramatically different from what you visualize?"

The Younger Facilitator responded, "Well, let me tell you the rest of the story. There I was in Thailand, fulfilling what I had imagined and designed, and suddenly something altered my vision. I experienced a tsunami that devastated the coastal village where I was staying. In the days following the disaster, people were in a state of shock, and I was surrounded by orphans who had lost their parents. Needless to say, my plans were altered; the experience I had envisioned was dramatically changed.

"It was like praying the **Prayer of Jabez**[60], really believing that great things are going to happen, and then things happen way beyond the scope of your imagination. Again, it was like believing in the power of serendipitous events that are supposed to happen to you via the law of attraction. Now the challenge is to find the meaning of the experience and respond with resources that you have.

"We all have experienced unique situations in life that we don't expect. The question is, how can you respond passionately with all the resources you have available? Passion attracts passion like the forces of magnets.

"My response to the situation was choosing to be passionate about using the resources available to me. In the short term, this meant I involved myself in a massive clean-up effort in the place where I was. In considering the long term, I asked myself, 'What resources are available to me?' The answer was that I had the experience, and I had the platform to share the story of what had happened. My long-term response involved raising funds by presenting slide shows about Thailand, rock climbing and the tsunami. Ultimately, I did this to support the orphans and people of Thailand in creating a better future.

"This is one example of creating passion and responding with passion. The question is, how can you apply these global strategies and create a formula that works for you?

"Remember, life is a continuous evolution of searching for strategies that work for you. If you are ready and if you are proactively seeking specific tools for specific purposes, then the 'teachers' or the tools will appear. Then it is up to you to embrace the message of the teacher, choose a few tools, and test and discover how they work.

"This takes time. You must consistently feed your body, mind and spirit with healthy food, oxygen, data, prayer, meditation, exercise, beliefs and positive thoughts, words and actions. And above all, embrace the present, because this is where passion exists.

"We must continually feed and nourish our own happiness and contentment in this life. King Solomon, one of the world's wisest men, said, 'It is a good and pleasant thing for one to eat and to drink, and to enjoy the good of all his labor that he takes to do under the sun all the days of his life.' We must individually discover the components of our work, relationships and the life we sense we must live — and joyfully manage the life we choose to live. To really see, hear and feel the lasting positive results in your life, you must commit to at least 12 months of concentrated effort in the growth zone."

Back in the classroom, the Older Facilitator added to the insights of the Younger Facilitator about passion and continuous personal evolution. "We mentioned earlier the process of reaching unconscious competence. Let me continue that process by explaining the Mastery Mountain model that describes how we can progress to that stage in every area of our lives.

MASTERY

UNCONSCIOUS COMPETENCE
CONSCIOUS COMPETENCE
CONSCIOUS INCOMPETENCE
UNCONSCIOUS INCOMPETENCE

UNCONSCIOUS CONFIDENCE
CONSCIOUS CONFIDENCE
CONSCIOUS UNCONFIDENCE
UNCONSCIOUS UNCONFIDENCE

"We begin in a stage of being completely unaware that a different or better way of doing something even exists; we are *unconsciously incompetent*. You don't even know that there is something to be aware of. I like to call this the 'completely clueless' phase. And that's okay: we all are in this phase at various points in our lives."

As the Older Facilitator moved to write again on the flip chart, Freedom interjected, "If we are all in this phase at some point, then how can we move out of this phase quickly when we need to learn something new?"

"Great question, Freedom. I like to say that feedback is the breakfast of champions. We need not only to be open to feedback but also to actively seek out feedback. When we have difficulty with or even fail at a task, we often find that there is something else to learn and know. Sometimes, someone will provide feedback to us, but we are not open to it, or we're too stubborn to listen; in either case, we won't hear the feedback, and we stay in unconscious incompetence. The best recommendation I can provide in this phase is **ask**[61]! Seek out information that others can provide. We all need to surround ourselves with a *support team*[62] of individuals who can and will provide that feedback. Let these people who are close to us at work and at home know that we are open to and expecting some good, candid feedback in the areas in which we seek to grow.

"Once we realize that there is something to learn or a skill that we need to acquire, we become *consciously incompetent*. We know what we *should* be doing, but don't yet know *how* to do it. At this stage, we must seek out those who are achieving the results we desire and *model after others' success*[63]. Remember, success leaves clues.

"Next, we become aware of that certain thing and realize that we need to acquire the skill set to actually do it. Practice! Remember the old saying, 'Repetition is the mother of Skill'? Well she had a little-known sister called Discipline. When we fail, learn and grow, and eventually learn the skill, we become *consciously competent*.

"Finally, as we climb to the summit of Competence Mountain, we have practiced the skill so much that we can do it without even thinking about it; we become *unconsciously competent*. Remember Aristotle's words on excellence? 'We are what we repeatedly do. Excellence then, is not an act, but a habit.'

"I want you all to continue to think about how you can progress through each one of those stages. How do you become aware of something you aren't aware of? Once you are aware, how do you learn and develop the skill you need? And what does it take to reach unconscious competence?"

The Older Facilitator nodded to the Younger Facilitator, who continued, "We all have different focus areas that are most important to us. Part of the process of Seeking True North is deciding what is

most important to you and progressing up through these stages to
the summit of Mastery Mountain.

"One way to identify what is most important to you is to
determine the roles that you play out on a continuous basis in your
life." The Younger Facilitator went on to explain a process called
the *Wheel of Life*[64]. During this process, participants identified and
wrote out personal and professional visions for the most important
areas to continually focus and improve upon.

He continued, "The other mountain you must climb in your
journey up Mastery Mountain is Confidence Mountain. The same
stages that apply to developing competence likewise apply to
developing confidence. As we increase our competencies, we are also
progressing naturally toward greater confidence. This is the point at
which we must choose a specific environment and test the theory so
that we can become more confident. This is where we must engage
our belief systems and affirmations to act as if we are ready and
capable to bridge the gap between theory and practice."

With a glance, the Younger Facilitator passed the floor, and the
Older Facilitator began to speak. "When we are in this process and
we fail at testing, how do we continue the process until we become
unconsciously confident? Stop the whining, blubbering, and sniveling,
and get your lazy butt back into action!"

Many participants gazed at the Older Facilitator with jaws
dropped and eyes wide. He gazed around the room and said with a
laugh, "This is the *Kick-butt Principle*[65], which I, of all people, need
the most." He raised his hand and said, "Anyone else need to do that,
or am I the only one?" They all laughed.

"Let me share three ways to determine our success," he went on.
"First, we have our tasks that we perform. We set out to accomplish
something, and along the way, we gain feedback on what we are
accomplishing. Second, we have our performance in the context of

social acceptance. Is what I am doing perceived by those around me as a valuable contribution to the society I live in? Those people whom we want to help with our contributions constitute our 'society,' which can be anywhere from local to global. A third way to determine our success comes from an internal gut sense. When we pay attention to our internal dialogue — the conjunction of body, mind and spirit — we can embrace a continuous process of positive self-evaluation. Together, body, mind and spirit provide a way to learn about positive changes we want to incorporate into our lives. In each of these methods of determining 'success,' we must continually focus on building confidence.

"As we travel this journey toward True North, remember that all of these principles of success are forged in the experiences of failure to achieve desired end results. We must do it, do it and do it again, continuing to build the confidence level we desire. We must maintain our belief systems and not let them falter in this testing, confidence-building process. We must each have a strong support system of people to assist us in this process — positive people who will encourage us to keep at it until our confidence grows to unconscious confidence.

"These two concepts of *competence* and *confidence* are critical to the process of developing mastery in every part of our lives. To reach Mastery Mountain, we must continually build strong self-confidence and self-competence as they relate to our desired end results.

"And let me make one more point — maybe the most important point of all — so listen carefully. We all need to have goals to inspire us to achieve the results we desire. However, the real goal in life must be about the process of learning through our experiences. When our definition of success is one of personal awareness and continuous learning, then we will always maintain and develop our personal power. Real success in life is this awareness of self in a context of continuous growth. Ultimately, your focus on the process will enable you to maintain passion in your life. When you do that, you will achieve the goals you set."

"The Older Facilitator speaks very wisely," commented the Younger Facilitator, stepping forward. "Remember that it is this process of awareness and learning that maintains passion as we continue Seeking True North. Now it is time to transition our enlightenment. It is very important to bring psychological and physiological closure to learning moments. Please, let us stand and form a Ready Circle.

"One of the ways we like to bring closure to a learning moment or learning day is to do what we call a **Word Send**[65]. As a team, we collectively agree on one word that we can send off into the universe. Remember, our actions are all set into motion by a word or a thought. So, team, what word do you choose to send?"

Considerable discussion arose. People started calling out words such as "teamwork," "prepare," "trust," and "values." There was some sharing about why someone chose this word or that. Finally, Freedom said, "I think we should send *passion*. Maybe for my own selfish reasons, because I so want to add more passion to my life at work, to my leadership responsibilities and to my relationships with my wife, family and friends."

"I want that, too," Beautiful agreed. "I agree with Freedom; I think we should send *passion*."

A gentle smile lit the face of the Younger Facilitator as he softly replied, "Well, we have a number of words selected, and the challenge was for you as a team to collectively decide on what one word you wanted to send now, at this moment. I will give you all 60 seconds to decide as a team and state your answer."

Several people spoke at once, calling out "Passion!" After a few seconds, one woman spoke again. "I think we have decided on the word passion."

"Is that it? Are you in agreement?" asked the Younger Facilitator. Everyone nodded. A few responded with "yes."

"Then move in closer to the center of the circle," the Younger Facilitator directed them. "Put your hands in the center, touching the hand of at least one other person. When I say the word 'practice', we are going to lift our hands slowly, firmly whisper the word 'passion,' and send it off into the universe. It will be there forever, for us to grab whenever we want or need it. Ready? Prepare, practice." With that, the group simultaneously lifted their hands and whispered, "Passion!"

Freedom walked back to his lodge to clean up before dinner, deep in thought. "I feel different," he thought. "Something positive really does seem to be going on here at this retreat — oops!" he chuckled. "I mean 'advance.' I hope it works."

✳ ✳ ✳

Later that evening, the entire group sat at dinner on the deck, taking in the perfect view of the gorgeous valley and mountains beyond. The sun was setting over the mountains, the temperature was perfect, the wine was poured, and an obvious positive energy was flowing in the room. Beautiful was seated at a round table with 11 other participants, the association's executive director and the Younger Facilitator.

At the other round table sat the remaining 12 participants, including Freedom, who was sitting directly across from the Older Facilitator. He glanced over at Beautiful, who just happened to look over at him at the exact same moment. Beautiful tilted her head and smiled. Freedom smiled. Lots of friendly conversation took place during dinner. Occasional laughter arose from each table. The words prepare, practice and passion were heard several times during the course of the evening as people connected and got to know each other. Before excusing themselves, the Older and Younger Facilitators said good night and encouraged everyone to stop and take a good look at the stars before going to bed.

This time, walking slowly back to his lodge, Freedom stared at the beautiful, twinkling stars, so bright they seemed to hang just above the Earth. He felt he could almost touch them and feel their energy. Just then, a brilliant shooting star burst into view from the south and shot over the mountains to the north. "Wow!" gasped Freedom. Then he laughed out loud. Freedom drew in a deep breath, sighed and then said, " Good night stars, goodnight moon, goodnight world."

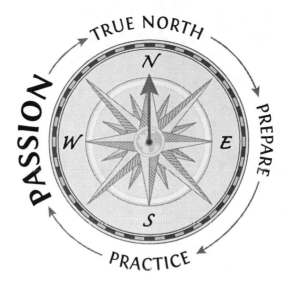

It Is Very Simple to Create Passion:

1. **Make a conscious decision to embrace the moment…**

   …and create happiness and meaning in your life.

2. **Surround yourself with positive people…**

   …and learn from the meaning of each experience.

3. **Feed your body, mind and spirit with positivity…**

   …and embrace the process with every step along your path.

Relationships

"Listen to the birds singing their morning songs. Look at the sunrise illuminating the mountain peaks. Breathe deeply and fill your lungs with the cool, clean air. Good morning, everyone. *Carpe Momento*[67]*!* Are you ready for *the most incredibly awesome day of your entire life*[68]? Okay, let's get the oxygen pumping and the blood flowing."

The Younger Facilitator began the morning session by explaining and demonstrating the *Breathwalk*[69]. Participants practiced this dynamic meditation technique, which combines breathing with specific walking patterns and directed mental focus. Following the Breathwalk, the group had a short debrief about how the technique can be used to clarify thoughts, boost energy and master emotional states throughout the day. Next, the Younger Facilitator led warm-up exercises in which the group moved in a circle while following various commands.

As the group settled, the Older Facilitator led the group in *macro and micro stretches*[70]. "Okay, who has another stretch for us?" he asked. "Is the next one a micro stretch or a macro stretch?"

One of the men spoke up. "Yes, it's my turn, and this stretch will be a clapping stretch." With that, he led the group in a variety of clapping rhythms. A woman led next, saying, "Now for a macro stretch. Get together with a partner, and we will do quad stretching."

"I have one last stretch for us before I turn things over to Mr. Younger Facilitator," said the older one. "This one is the most natural of all stretches. It's called the *laughter stretch*[71]." Freedom and Beautiful glanced at each other, puzzled but curious. "It all starts with a little giggle. Come on, giggle with me." People looked around, and curious smiles led to small giggles.

"Okay, let's pick it up a little to a nice chuckle. Everyone chuckle!" The group followed suit, and the laughter rose steadily in volume and heartiness. "Okay now, the full-blown laugh. Make it the knee-slapping, hurt-your-ribs, tears-in-your-eyes hysteria!" The laughter was so hearty that people were in shock as to how funny it was. As the laughter continued, Freedom turned to Beautiful and managed to say, "I feel like a kid again. I'd forgotten how good it feels to laugh, laugh, laugh!"

The Younger Facilitator then said, "Let's close our session this morning and open our day with a clear mind. I want you to sit comfortably, close your eyes and focus on your breathing. Clear your mind with the smooth rhythms of your breath. Let all those thoughts about other people, responsibilities and distractions just float away. If a thought enters your mind, acknowledge it, repeat it and let it go. For example, if work enters your mind, simply say 'work' a few times and let the thought drift off. Refocus your breathing and clear your mind."

The group sat in silence, breathing and meditating for the next five minutes. "Slowly open your eyes, look at your surroundings and those near you, and open your heart. Fully embrace each moment of the day and prepare for the fact that today is going to be the most incredible day of your entire life." They ended the morning session with more visualization and *meditation*[72] while gazing at the serene mountain vistas.

The Older Facilitator broke the silence. "I want you to think about the *meaning of this day*[73]. We all have the power to create associations with each experience we share. For one, it may be opening your heart and mind to a new way of thinking. For another, it might be a positive affirmation that we are being proactive in discovering the tools we need to be happier in life. What is the meaning of this day for you?"

The Younger Facilitator concluded the session with inspirational comments. "You all have the potential to achieve whatever you desire in this world. Realize, as you travel on your pathway, that the relationships you develop and maintain along the way can be your greatest source of inspiration — or frustration. Over the rest of our time together, we will explore this core of what Seeking True North is all about. Please point to the highest mountains and repeat after me, with gusto, *'To infinity and beyond*[74]*!*. They all said it with robust voices and then laughed.

Getting on the small tour shuttle, Freedom scanned the bus for a seat. Halfway down the aisle on the right sat Beautiful. He felt a little nervous but walked down the aisle and asked, "May I sit with you, Beautiful?"

Beautiful smiled and replied, "Sure, Freedom. That would be great."

Freedom suddenly dropped his notebook and backpack, fumbled to catch them, and nearly poked one of the other participants in the eye. "I am sooo sorry," he stammered. Beautiful covered her mouth to hide her giggling.

Freedom noticed this and thought, "God, I am such a dork. I am such a loser!" After gathering his stuff together, Freedom sat down and again apologized to Beautiful and the others around him. They all told him it was no problem, and the man across the aisle even put in a funny reminder that Freedom had "almost" poked him in the eye while being a "Mop Woman Wannabe." They all laughed.

Once all were on board, they headed through town toward the mountains for a day of light hiking and outdoor workshop sessions.

A few minutes into the ride, the Younger Facilitator announced on the microphone, "Let's give a hearty, rousing welcome to our shuttle driver and guide." As cheers and applause broke out, the Younger Facilitator gave a hearty endorsement: "Yes, that's what we want to hear."

As they rode toward the mountains, the Younger and Older Facilitators led the group in an interactive game to share *fun facts*[75] about the history of the area, the many species of birds and mammals, the resorts and more. Each person had been handed some of these facts on slips of paper as he or she boarded the shuttle. Then the facilitators took turns asking if someone had a fact about this or that. At various times, individual participants grabbed the microphone and shared a fact while practicing public speaking skills. After each speaker finished, the entire group responded by applauding and celebrating the individual's "Practice."

The scenery seemed to become more beautiful the closer they got to their hiking destination. After some casual conversation about their respective homes and work, Beautiful asked Freedom, "What are your thoughts about the advance so far?"

Freedom took a deep breath and sighed. "I like it so far. To be honest, I came here as a 'Prisoner,'" he said, quirking his fingers to signal quotation marks. "But I have definitely moved toward becoming a 'Leader.' I only hope that I can use these tools to make a lasting, positive difference in my life. How about you, Beautiful? What are your thoughts about the advance?"

Just then, the shuttle pulled over into a small parking area, and the Younger Facilitator announced that this was the forest where they would spend the day. "Let's hold that thought and plan to sit together on the way home so I can answer your question," said Beautiful. "Does that sound okay with you?"

"Sounds great to me," replied Freedom with a smile.

Before departing the shuttle, the facilitators handed out *information cards*[76] — index cards with some information printed on them. The Younger Facilitator announced through the microphone, "Please partner with the person you are sitting with. While walking on the trail, you and your partner will read your individual cards. Share with each other how the information on your card relates to you in your life. The information is directly related to the book that you were assigned to read or listen to on CD before you arrived here for the advance."

Before heading up the trail, they were instructed as a team to *create a system*[77] for distributing their packs, water and food, and to gather in a Ready Circle in a small meadow just a few yards into the woods.

When they had gathered, the Older Facilitator, in his usual confident speaking stance, glanced around the circle and smiled at each person. "First, I have to acknowledge your leader and executive director for teaching me how to have such a powerful *speaking stance*[78]. He taught me this several years ago, and it has proved to be incredibly beneficial in my life. You would do well to practice it yourself until it becomes an unconscious competence in your life." With this, the Older Facilitator turned to the executive director, bowed with folded hands and said, "I thank you again."

They smiled at each other. Then, one by one, each participant practiced public speaking in the form of a two-minute presentation on their information card and the application to their workforce development. The Younger Facilitator added a suggestion that they all join their local *Toastmasters*[79] public speaking clubs in their respective hometowns.

The Older Facilitator closed the segment with another piece of advice: "To foster continuous growth in our workplaces, I want to add here a suggestion that in your workplace you set up a library. Have

mandatory book reading and CD listening[80] every quarter. Everyone studies the same book or CD, thus building on a foundation to create synergy and practice using common tools and skills learned from the quarterly studies. In an organized session, everyone shares and discusses what they have learned and how to apply it in their lives. Ongoing, concentrated growth using the same source will produce shared situational awareness of the learning and will produce positive results in any group of people."

The Older Facilitator paused to look up at a bird perched on a branch and then continued. "When I say 'Shikaka,' I want you to look and point at someone across the circle from you. Act as if you are very surprised to see him or her here, inhale a quick, loud breath, and repeat whatever I say with enthusiasm. Ready? Shikaka!"

With that, everyone looked at someone else, took a deep startling breath, and pointed as the Older Facilitator said, ***"I can't believe..."***[81].

They all enthusiastically responded, "I can't believe!"

The Older Facilitator continued, "That I am in..."

At once, all said, "That I am in!"

"...the same woods..."

"The same woods!"

"...with a leader like you!"

"With a leader like you!"

"You are incredible!" ended the Older Facilitator.

"You are incredible!" came the response. Everyone laughed.

"I am giving you an assignment. When you get home, I want you to walk up to your children, look them in the eyes, take that deep startling breath, and say with enthusiasm, 'I can't believe...that I live... in the same house...with a person like you! You are incredible!'"

Everyone laughed again.

"Then," the Older Facilitator continued, "I want you to go to your spouse or significant other and say the same thing, making sure that you put the deep breath in, too. And remember, it's the big smile, the fun, laughter and passion in the sharing that creates the positive impact."

One of the participants immediately said, "If I do that, my wife is going to ask me what I have been drinking!" They all laughed and agreed.

"Isn't it sad that we are under suspicion for doing incredibly good things?" the Older Facilitator asked. "The reason for that is that most of us do not normally do incredibly good things in our average ordinary day here on planet Earth. I challenge you to begin doing more and more incredibly good things in your average ordinary day, with all the people you are connected with. Embrace random acts of kindness and make a point to make someone's moment. It might just make their day! Make it your 'norm.' Make it your unconscious competence to live out incredibly awesome moments, each and every day of your life. And share that abundance of wealth with everyone you meet. It is possible.

"What we say to others has a tremendous impact on them," he continued. "Our *self talk*[(82)] — what we say to ourselves, either out loud or internally — molds our perception of an experience and has tremendous influence in our lives. We should never say things to ourselves like 'I am such a loser!' or 'I am so stupid!' Such negative messages must be eliminated from our lips and minds."

Considering the Older Facilitator's words, Freedom asked, "Do you have any tools for how to do *that*?"

The Older Facilitator responded with another question: "How many of you have little voices in your head? Although we might not readily admit it, we all do. These are the thoughts that lead us to the actions we do or do not take. Sometimes there is one little voice, and sometimes there are more. Often, our little voices have conversations with each other. The key to eliminating negative thought processes is to **become a witness**[83] to those conversations. As you pay attention to those conversations in your mind, determine whether those thoughts are beneficial to a peaceful, productive state of mind, or not. As a witness to your mind, you increase your awareness of thoughts and are able to begin eliminating negative patterns."

Freedom paid close attention.

"There is an old-timer who has taught many to say to themselves, 'Life is Tremendous!' And it's true! Another has taught us to answer the question 'How are you today?' with 'I am **doing fantastically —and getting better**[84]!' Use that one from now on every time you go through the grocery store line as the checkout person generically asks you how you are.

"And if you really want to have a paradigm shift, go **backwards shopping**[85], where you push your grocery cart from the front, opposite the handle side, the entire time you are shopping. I guarantee you will get some looks. The experience is worth the experiment in attaching new meaning to your shopping experience and as a metaphor in shifting one action to produce an entirely different result."

The Older Facilitator announced the group's next challenge. "When I say 'Prepare,' I want you to form an arrow with your bodies in a standing position, and point to where you think **True North**[86] is. Make the main shaft of an arrow along with the two parts of an arrowhead point. You are not permitted to talk during this activity. You have 60 seconds to perform your task."

He paused, looked around, then said, "Ready? Prepare!" There was a bit of confusion and scrambling. A few people started pointing in one direction. Some pointed in another direction while maneuvering others into position.

"Ten seconds left," the Older Facilitator announced. There was some last-second shifting and directing by two individuals as the group maneuvered the arrow formation to where they thought True North was.

"Now," said the Older Facilitator, "if you think you are lined up correctly, pointing to True North, listen for me to say, 'Practice.' Please, then, with no talking, use your thumb-check assessment tool and give me thumbs up. If you think you need a bit of position adjustment, then put your thumbs to the side. If you think you are flat-out facing the wrong direction, then give me thumbs down. Ready? Practice!"

All hands went up in the air. Some thumbs were up. Some were down, and some were to the side. "Now *scan the group*[87] and look around you at the position of the thumbs," instructed the Older Facilitator. "When I say the word 'Passion,' I am going to give you 60 seconds to talk and brainstorm and adjust your arrow, if you desire to do so. Ready? Passion!"

Immediately and simultaneously, many voices broke the silence, each with an opinion. Realizing they were getting nowhere fast, Freedom quickly grabbed the train whistle from the hand of a startled Younger Facilitator and blew the whistle.

Everyone stopped talking and looked at Freedom. "I'm not good at directions," he said quickly, "but since we have only a few seconds to decide, I think we should find out who among us feels the most confident, based on experience in the woods and having a sense of direction, and listen to their direction."

They all quickly agreed. One man said he met the requirements and gave his opinion, and they all agreed to shift just a few degrees from their present positions.

The Older Facilitator stepped up to the front of the arrow with a compass in hand.

He showed it to the front person at the point of the arrow, who happened to be Beautiful, and said, "Very good. You are very close to pointing at True North. Give yourselves a round of applause."

Cheers of "Yes!" broke out, and all applauded.

The Older Facilitator stepped up on a boulder so that he was able to look at each person in the arrow and said, "Please, gather around and find a seat on these boulders here in the circle."

Freedom and Beautiful sat next to each other on some rocks just to the right of the Older Facilitator. After they were seated, the Younger Facilitator passed around a backpack and instructed each person to take a compass out of the pack. "These are yours to keep," he said. "Treat yours with care and use it as a *talisman*[88] as you travel on your pathway."

Then the Older Facilitator took a stick and drew a circle in the sandy, dusty soil where all could see. When he was finished and was seated on his rock, he said, "Your Younger Facilitator and I are licensed guides in rock climbing, hiking and camping. We spend a lot of time in the woods, on the rocks and in nature, during all four seasons." He paused and then said, "I get lost a lot — in the woods and in life." The group smiled, sensing his humor. "So far, though, I have always been able to find my way back to the pathway toward home. Mostly because my desired end result was to get back home but also because I knew in what direction I had to go, and I had the necessary tools and skills to arrive home.

"It is the same way in all of life. If you clearly know where you want to end up and you have the right tools and skills, then, even if you get off track, you can quickly return to the right pathway to your desired end result. It is this way for the mariner at sea, the pilot in the air and the geese and monarch butterflies migrating north and south. As we are seeking True North, some of the questions we must ask ourselves are:

Do I know what direction I am going in?

Do I know my desired end result?

Do I know why I want this desired end result?

Do I know what my values are, and what is most important to me along the way?

Am I monitoring my progress along the pathway?

Do I know what and where True North is in my life?"

"Most of my troubles come," he went on, "when I have not clearly defined what I want in regard to outcomes and process. For example, it is important to decide how much money I want to make each year and how I am going to manage it. If I do not joyfully manage my money, then my finances can quickly become out of control, and the resulting chaos produces frustration and potential disaster in my life. I must determine my desired end results in the realm of *financial literacy*[89] and the money I produce and manage.

"And more trouble comes when I do not have my body, mind and spirit in balance with the relationships in my life. Look at your compass. See the arrow on your base platform? This is simply an arrow that you can point toward an object you want to reach. The letter *N* on your compass stands for 'North.' And see the needle with a point on it? If you want to go north, you must line up the needle with the *N*. Of course, for you technical people, I know there is a difference between Magnetic North, Survey North and True North. But such technical distinctions do not affect the purpose of this exercise.

"The purpose of this activity is to explore how we choose to guide our lives, decisions, bodies, minds, spirits and relationships. What is our internal and external compass? When I clearly know the answer to these questions, I can lead more effectively, sell more effectively, manage more effectively, be happier and healthier, and have more meaningful relationships."

The Older Facilitator stood and began to write in the dirt again. He printed the letters *N, S, E* and *W* at four locations in the circle. Then he drew an arrow in the circle pointing to the N. Next, he wrote words at four locations inside the circle. At the E, he wrote the word Body. At the S, he wrote the word Mind. At the W, he wrote the word Spirit. Finally, at the N he wrote the word Relationships.

"This is your next tool. It can serve as a *life compass*[90] for you for the rest of your life, in all that you do. Each of the four elements is lined up with the four directions on the compass. We must seek the lifelong mastery of being healthy in body, mind and spirit. We have the unlimited power, potential, tools and resources to achieve this. And we must seek the lifelong mastery of healthy, meaningful relationships.

"Always remember, 100 percent of what we do in this life is relationship oriented in some way, shape or form. Relationships are at the core of money, work, family and community, and are the very core of life and love."

Freedom thought about his feelings of imbalance as a leader, manager and husband. He began to realize that maybe this was the reason he was not completely happy at work and at home. He thought about what the Older Facilitator had said. He realized that, at the core of his being, his internal and external compass arrows were not balanced with each other. He thought, "I am surrounded by tools and resources, but I have not clearly defined my desired end results while maintaining balance in the process. They all have to be working together in the right proportions." He felt a little tired and wished he could be free of this imbalance in his life.

The Older Facilitator continued, "This True North compass is something that we need to revisit continually to ensure a healthy balance in work, family and personal life. For the rest of your life, use your compass as a reminder to maintain a healthy balance in all of these facets of *Seeking True North*."

Over the next half hour, the group worked together, exploring what True North was for their association. Then they explored True North for their individual spheres of influence at home and work. At the suggestion of one participant, they all formed an arrow pointing north. Finally, they closed their learning session with a word send. Simultaneously, they shouted the word balance.

For the rest of that beautiful, sunny day at the base of the mountains, the participants engaged in fun, challenging activities. They all enjoyed an experiential team leadership event using *GPS devices*[91], two-way radios and a series of clues to solve a major challenge. The challenge was metaphorical for increased profits, sales and customer satisfaction in their businesses.

Another activity focused specifically on *building trust*[92]. During one of the breaks on the trail, the Younger Facilitator gathered a few nature enthusiasts and, of all things, gave a crash course on *identifying animal feces and tracks*[93]. Some of the participants were disgusted at the dissecting of dried feces and chose instead to engage in *balancing rocks*[94] with the association director and the Older Facilitator.

To cap off the day, they all hiked up a trail to a 40-foot cliff where, with the help of professional rock climbers, they practiced *rappelling*[95] off the cliff side by side with a partner. Before the rappel, each person had to privately choose an area of life that he or she wanted to force growth in. Then, at the bottom of the cliff, each shared the chosen growth goal and plans to achieve it.

Freedom and Beautiful decided to rappel together. Sharing at the bottom of the cliff, they realized that they had many similar goals. They both wanted to be more confident, happy and balanced in their lives.

On the trail back to the shuttle, the participants were instructed to form groups of three and discuss the events of the day. Taking a head count before hiking back to the shuttle, they noticed Freedom was missing. "I'm his safety buddy," said one of the men. "He is over in the woods just off the trail looking at the lake."

Just then, Freedom came out of the woods. Everyone else was in his or her trio. The Older Facilitator gestured to the Younger Facilitator and said, "Freedom, I guess you are stuck with us for the walk back."

"Oh good, I get to hang out with the top dogs," Freedom blurted out.

"Don't get cocky about it," responded the Older Facilitator. Freedom felt panicked inside. "Why did he say such a thing?" he thought to himself. He looked over at the Older Facilitator, only to find that he was grinning at Freedom.

"You need to have tougher skin," the Older Facilitator said as he poked Freedom in the arm and then patted him reassuringly on the shoulder.

Freedom breathed a sigh of relief.

The Younger Facilitator grinned and added, "Yes, Bumblebee Tuna! And don't forget to smile and have a little fun in your life, okay? Really, give yourself permission to have some fun. Let's say it together now: 'I give myself permission to have a blast in life.'"

All three repeated the statement and laughed together.

"So, Freedom," asked the Younger Facilitator. "What has been the highlight of your day so far?"

Freedom responded, "I have enjoyed everything, but if I had to choose one thing it would be the True North activity and tool. It was not my most fun highlight, but it was the most valuable."

"I see. I hear you. I have a sense for what you are saying," replied the Younger Facilitator.

"I have noticed that you two say that a lot. Why is that?" asked Freedom.

"Say what?" the Younger Facilitator asked.

"You say, 'I see. I hear. And I have a sense for.' Why do you say that?"

The Younger Facilitator laughed and said, "You'll find out tomorrow."

As they walked along the trail, they discussed the day's events, and the two facilitators asked Freedom about his family, home life and work. After some conversation, laughs and a few stops to observe some deer, the Older Facilitator asked Freedom, "Is your marriage and family life really healthy?"

Freedom was surprised at the personal question, but he responded, "I want my marriage and family life to be better.

Confidentially, I am not as happy as I want to be, and I think it is mainly my fault."

"How do you mean?" the Older Facilitator asked.

Sighing, Freedom said, "I think — no, I know — that I have some insecurity about not being an effective leader and manager at work and about my role as a husband and father. I've been trying a few tools, as you call them, but I can't seem to break through to new growth that lasts."

Freedom's mind was churning intently. These facilitators seemed so happy. He knew deep down that if he could feel happy more often, then he would feel free. "So, I want to know about happiness. I have to know: How do you both stay so happy all the time?"

The Older and Younger Facilitator glanced at each other and smiled. The Older Facilitator nodded to the Younger Facilitator, and the Younger Facilitator began. "Happiness is a state — a state of being that encompasses how you think and feel at any given moment. You can create and experience happiness at any given moment in your life. To be content in life is to be satisfied with how much happiness you have on an ongoing basis. And personally, I think deep joy comes from a sense of internal peace."

The Older Facilitator nodded. "Many people think of happiness as an outcome in life. They say, 'I will be happy when...' and fill in the blank with every material objective imaginable. Now achieving your desired end results is important, but you must remember that seeking and maintaining happiness, meaning, peace and joy is a continuous evolution. It's about the process — the journey."

The Younger Facilitator spoke up again. "Yes, there must be a balance, which allows you to continually enjoy and celebrate the process as you set and achieve important goals in your life. We become free when we are able to live in, be at peace with and embrace the present moment."

Smiling, the Older Facilitator added, "As you continue along your journey Seeking True North, achieving your desired end results, you must remember to hold true to your values and beliefs. Of course, that means you have to know what those values and beliefs are! I call that process of knowing and applying those values and beliefs, *Climbing Myself Mountain*[96]."

"I get it," Freedom replied. "But how is one person happy with an experience, and another person not happy with that same experience?"

"Good question, Freedom," the Older Facilitator responded. "Remember that with each experience, we have the ability to create its meaning. In every moment in life, we are deciding what that experience means. Failure to one person is learning, or success, to another. Remember that you can always reframe your experience in a way that is positive and that will facilitate your success in the future."

"We all make poor decisions at times," the Younger Facilitator added, "and often get poor results. But you know what? *Acceptance*[97] of our decisions is key to maintaining a state of peace and harmony. We must trust that our benevolent decisions are the best decisions we can make at the time. And the real question is, what can we learn from the decisions we make?

"We cannot go back and change the past. We *can* reflect on those decisions and learn from them. Such acceptance and reflection enable us to reduce the stress and worry that many of us focus on when we harbor guilt or resentment. And the friends we surround ourselves with can help us see alternative perspectives. An experience that may seem awful initially may turn out to be very positive. You never know. Happiness to me is doing all I can to create and achieve my desired end results, and accepting and learning from my failures along the way."

Freedom concluded, "And as you go along achieving, you are using your core values and beliefs to guide your decisions to maintain a positive state of mind and being."

"Very well said, Freedom," acknowledged the Older Facilitator.

Freedom smiled inside and began thinking about how he would begin to apply what the facilitators were obviously living out in their daily lives. Then he asked, "You two seem so passionate, as you call it, about what you do. How do you do that?"

The Younger Facilitator replied while glancing at Freedom and the Older Facilitator. "As far as I'm concerned, the foundation for passion and for success in life is a strong, positive attitude."

"Yes," agreed the Older Facilitator. "And that positive attitude must be consistently and publicly demonstrated."

"Your attitude is determined by your focus," the Younger Facilitator continued. "If you make being passionate a focus in your life, then your attitude and actions shift. It is safe to say that we decided to love life and be passionate not only in pursuing the specific end results we desire, but also in embracing the process along the way. When I really want to be something or do something, I make a decision that I am willing to die for. It's like Abraham Lincoln, Martin Luther King Jr. or Mother Theresa. They were all passionate about their desired end results, and all were willing to die for what they believed they should be doing on planet Earth."

"Do you think the same as well?" Freedom asked, turning to the Older Facilitator.

"Yes," he replied softly.

The three walked down the trail in silence for some time. Finally, the Older Facilitator asked, "So, Freedom, why do you do what you do? And, how do you know when you are successful?"

He asked the question so casually, as if you would ask someone about the weather, that Freedom felt a little nervous and slightly puzzled. He pondered the questions and wondered if he had heard correctly. But he knew he had. He did not want to reply because he knew he did not fully know the answers. "These facilitators are deep," he thought. "They seem to live so passionately, but it seems that for them living passionately is as easy as walking down this trail in the woods." Freedom responded, "I can't fully answer those questions right now. Give me some time to think about it."

"Sure," replied the Older Facilitator.

Freedom added, "I can tell you right now that I am going to try to do some of the things that you have been teaching us."

The Older Facilitator grinned and replied, "That's great, Freedom. Let me tell you a story about 'trying.' On that beautiful fall day I mentioned earlier, when the Younger Facilitator and I were rock climbing together, we came upon a large overhanging section of the route. As I held his life-line belay rope and watched him climb up and over the roof in the cliff, doubt filled my mind. I stared at the Younger Facilitator and yelled up to him, 'I don't know! Those moves look hard! I am not sure if I can do it, but I'll give it a try!'

"The Younger Facilitator was just pulling over the rooftop, through the most difficult section, or crux as climbers call it, when I called. He stopped, stared back at me, and stated very clearly, 'Master Facilitator, there is no try — only do, or do not do. So, which will it be?'

"In that moment, I made a decision — a decision to do. And I have to tell you, making it up that cliff was an incredible, rewarding experience. Now I don't 'try,' I 'do.' It's what we call the **Yoda factor**[98]."

On the way back to the resort, the facilitators suggested **varying partners**[99]; they each had to choose a different partner to sit beside. Beautiful passed by Freedom in the aisle on the shuttle and said, "I guess we'll have to finish our conversation at another time."

They played a game called **Two Truths and One Lie**(100), in which they tried to fool one another with fun facts about their own lives. Lots of laughs passed the time, and they had barely finished the game when they arrived back at the resort. The association director announced, "I'll see you all at seven o'clock for the barbeque dinner and the billiard tournament."

* * *

Beautiful was enjoying the social interaction and fun of the billiard tournament, but in her thoughts, she was pondering the day. She thought of her relationship with her husband. She truly loved him and wanted their love to grow and be richer and more fulfilling. But she had this nagging feeling all the time that she was not beautiful enough.

Sometimes her husband's words seemed so abusive. She longed to be content with herself. This longing within her to know she was really loved and appreciated seemed to constantly tug at her. She wanted to be more confident in herself. "If I could just do that," she thought, "I think I could be a happier wife, a better mom and a more effective manager."

She looked over and saw the Older Facilitator sitting at one of the small tables by himself. So, she went over and asked, "May I join you?"

"Of course, Beautiful," he replied after he had swallowed a bite of his catfish burrito.

"I really am enjoying my time here," said Beautiful. "It is proving to be very valuable to me. More than I ever expected."

"I am so glad for you, Beautiful," the Older Facilitator replied. "It is a very valuable time for me, as well. I am learning new things this week about myself that are forcing me into the growth zone once again!"

They looked at each other and laughed.

Beautiful suddenly became more serious, moved her stool a little closer and said, "I feel I can trust you with something confidential about myself that I want to talk about. Is that okay with you?"

The Older Facilitator looked her in the eyes and studied her for a moment, then replied, "A law of the order of freedom in the Universe is that everything must have **boundaries**[101]. I'll tell you when to stop if I feel I cannot talk with you about your concerns. Is that okay with you?"

Beautiful managed a little smile and said, "Deal." She continued, "I'll get right to the point because we don't have a lot of time, and catching you alone is a difficult task. I love my husband and want to be with him for all my life, but sometimes he can be so hurtful with his words. The other thing is, I was abused as a child, and all my life I have struggled with not feeling really loved or beautiful enough." A tear trickled down her cheek as she managed to choke out these last few words.

The Older Facilitator looked at her and gently smiled. He and Beautiful talked for some minutes, and finally he asked her, "Do you ever speak hurtful words to your husband?"

"Yes," she replied. "I am guilty of that."

After a pause for thought, the Older Facilitator said, "I think we all need to be healed of something that is painful in our lives. I don't know how to heal people. Sometimes I wish I had that power, but then I might not know when I should heal someone and when not to. As for you not feeling beautiful, I too have struggled with that in my life."

"Really?" Beautiful replied. "But you are so handsome."

"Yes, me, really!" he answered. "And thanks for the complement. I know I am handsome, but it is good to hear it from a beautiful woman like you." They laughed together. "Yes, growing up, I was a freckle-faced, dorky kid lacking in self-confidence and full of middle-child insecurities."

"I was thinking more about internal beauty," said Beautiful. "So how did you become so confident on the inside and know that you are beautiful — I mean, handsome — too?" asked Beautiful.

"I had to convince myself," replied the Older Facilitator. "No one could do it for me.

"People all around the world are hurting, some from being abused, some as victims of war, some from depression because of uncertainty in this world and in their lives. Most people live out of their memory and their focus is on the past. It is much healthier if we embrace the now, and live our lives in the present as we create a healthy future.

"As for the specifics of how I began my journey of healing, I will answer by giving you some of the foundational advice that I was given by a wise woman in my village.

"Keep in mind that *your* progress in growth and development will be unique to you. As you consider your current situation, realize that you have **three choices**[102]. You can remove yourself from the situation, change it or fully embrace it. Many people wait around, begging God for a miracle to bring about change in their lives in the future. I think it is better to say, 'Okay, Lord, bless me indeed, and help me bring about the change I desire. Let's see if we can create a miracle together.' You must constantly practice by filling your thinking data banks, your mind, with great thoughts of how beautiful and special you are. Never stop doing this.

"You can begin by writing out your 100 goals and, as we talked about earlier, recording affirmations in your own voice. Review your goals periodically and listen to your affirmations all the time. Go on an all-out war against anything that tries to tell you that you are not beautiful and valuable to God, yourself, your spouse, your family and your friends. Live a passionate life and keep yourself in peak physical, mental and spiritual shape.

"If you realize that there is something you are not receiving in a relationship, then focus on giving that certain thing. There is freedom, beauty and success in love. You must seek to know and love yourself better so you can become healthier and share your love with others. Always remember that you are the best person you can be in the moment that you are living; feel peace by understanding that you are always making the best decisions at the moment you are making them. "Lastly, remember *the law of attraction*[103]. We attract everything we receive in life. What we attract is what we focus on. When you start focusing on what you want, instead of what you don't want, the universe will respond. Embrace what you want, and realize that there is no limit to what we can achieve.

"Those were the words of wisdom from the wise woman in my village. I would like to challenge you to consider how the tools of preparation, practice, and passion apply specifically to your situation. I could give you a lot more homework — there are many more facets to healing — but for now, I will give you just one more assignment.

"You are already a leader who influences people around you in a positive way. And you are already 'Beautiful.' Go on a mission to help others become beautiful and strong, positive leaders. I guarantee that when you commit to helping others become what you have had to learn to become, you will find yourself being more beautiful than you ever thought possible. You are what is called a *Wounded Healer*[104]. I know, because I am one too."

Beautiful fought back tears and looked at the Older Facilitator, who was smiling at her.

They hugged. The Older Facilitator held her by the shoulders and said enthusiastically, "Let's play some pool!"

* * *

The next day of the advance was just as great as the days before. The participants prepared, practiced and were passionate about working on a healthy balance of body, mind, spirit and relationships. The concept of Seeking True North was brought up over and over in many of the challenges, tools and initiatives.

People shared how they planned to use these new tools in their management, leadership, sales, customer relations, and more importantly, in their personal, spiritual and family lives. On the shuttle to the mountains, the Younger Facilitator smiled and said, "One of the most valuable time-management strategies is called *The Seven Most Important Things*[105]." He went on to explain the process of planning and prioritizing each day to accomplish one's most important objectives.

Resting from their hike next to a gorgeous, serene lake, the group soaked in the mirror reflection of the trees and mountains. The Older Facilitator led them in several activities to practice *matching visual, auditory and kinesthetic (VAK) communication styles*[106], the three predominant means of communication and rapport-building.

"We are born programmed to think predominantly in one of these three styles of communication. To be more effective in all of our relationships with customers, co-workers, friends and loved ones close to our hearts, we must practice using all three methods. We will all become more successful in building rapport with others as we learn how to shift into another person's style when communicating. It takes a little practice, but it is not that difficult to recognize when another person is thinking and speaking in visual, auditory or kinesthetic language. This is why you have heard us say 'see, hear and experience' so often. Then, very simply, your goal is to match the other person's communication style. This is a very powerful method of building rapport quickly."

The facilitators presented another experiential challenge that involved creating a safe way for all to *cross a river*[107] using only natural resources. The activity led to a discussion about teamwork and how to create a safe culture and environment at home and in the workplace. The Younger Facilitator interjected the *GRIP model*[108], in which the team analyzed group goals, roles, interpersonal interactions and process efficiency. Throughout the day, the group practiced catching people doing "right" and complimenting them.

A surprise wet snowfall threw an unexpected beauty and challenge into the day. Much synergy, *celebration and fun*[109] took place, including another hilariously energizing Laughter Stretch. This energy was noticed even more at lunch when Beautiful and Freedom teamed up and started throwing snowballs at the association director. That led to a huge, raucous, all-out snowball war that lasted quite some time.

A rare treat was having the Older Facilitator teach them *generalized principles in nature*[110]. "There are many principles and laws in nature that can benefit us in our creativity. Buckminster Fuller knew this when he discovered the engineering for the Geodesic Dome. Franklin knew it when playing with the power of electricity. We would all do well to slow down and pay attention to the simplistic generalized principles in nature to assist us in our lives."

He followed this session by showing them how to put their ears against a tree that had another tree leaning against it, and listen to the loud squeak of the trees rubbing against each other. To hear this sound traveling inside the trunk of the tree was incredible. They saw lots of deer, eagles, a coyote and even a moose!

Walking the trail back to the shuttle, Beautiful had a chance to share her thoughts about the advance experience with Freedom.

"Someone once asked me if I could freely dance as if no one were watching. At the time, I could not. But as I reflect on everything, I feel as though I am ready. I am beginning to really believe in myself and that I am on a new path to discovering my purpose and potential in life. Not just for a short time, but for the rest of my life. This stuff is real. I feel it. I know it."

On the shuttle ride home, the Older Facilitator led the group in the *Damper Song*[(111)], which got the groups, once again, laughing and having fun. One by one they stood and practiced their public-speaking techniques by sharing their favorite inspirational *leadership quotes*[(112)].

That evening, they enjoyed a trip to a local museum for dinner and a program on changing perspectives through exploration of the arts.

Later that night, Freedom lay in bed considering all the events of the past three days. He sensed positive changes coming to him in his life. As he drifted off to sleep, Freedom's last thoughts were, "Tomorrow is going to be one of the most incredibly awesome days of my entire life."

* * *

Looking out the window of the conference room the next morning, the participants could see the sun illuminating the mountains. They all sat in a Ready Circle, filled with positive expectations for the closing of the advance.

Freedom and Beautiful sat next to each other as the Younger and Older Facilitators stood at the front of the group, just as they had three days before, at the opening session. The Older Facilitator gathered the attention of the group. "Welcome to the closing session of our time together," he said. "This is your opportunity to review the concepts and tools that we have been sharing over the past few days. Who can share a model, method or tool that we have covered here together?"

And then, one by one, the participants shared their insights from the Seeking True North Advance. Comments flowed as they expressed how they would put them into practice. As each comment was shared, the Facilitators summarized the topic by writing a few words on the flip charts. Soon enough, the wall was covered with all the concepts that the group had learned.

The Younger Facilitator announced, "Now it is time to transfer your knowing what to do, to doing what you know." The facilitators instructed the group in the mechanics of several goal-setting and action-planning models. They practiced *action planning*[113], *storyboarding*[114] and setting *SMART goals*[115]; and each participant wrote a *self-addressed letter*[116] as reminders of their personal agreements. The group also chose *accountability partners*[117] to follow up with in the upcoming weeks and months. Of course, Freedom and Beautiful agreed to partner with each other to reinforce their commitments to implement what they had learned.

Just as the partner conversations were ending, the Younger Facilitator opened the door. A lively chocolate Labrador Retriever came bounding into the middle of the circle, wagging his tail and investigating the group. "Telos!" said the Younger Facilitator with a pleasant, welcoming voice. "Ladies and gentleman, I would like to introduce you to Telos, my lifelong friend."

Telos, upon hearing his name, turned to the Younger Facilitator and cocked his head sideways. Just then, Beautiful spoke up. "What does Telos mean again?"

"Does anyone remember?" the Younger Facilitator asked.

Freedom answered, "Telos means purpose."

"Very good, Freedom. Now for Telos here, he is achieving his purpose just by being himself. Bounding through the woods, chasing after small animals, fetching balls and being the most loyal companion you can imagine. As we all move from this place back into our daily lives, I want you all to think about your Telos. Why are you here? For what purpose? What is your true potential? What legacy will you leave?"

Telos stood up, shook his sleek brown body, and moved to lie down next to the association director. They all had warm, thoughtful smiles on their faces. Freedom thought, "It seems that as we continue Seeking True North in our own lives through Preparation, Practice and Passion, we will be living our Telos."

"Now it is time to close our advance with The Gift." The Younger Facilitator then shared a quote: "Yesterday is history, tomorrow a mystery, today is a gift, that's why we call it the present." One by one, people shared small gifts with the person each had been assigned to secretly watch and catch doing "right."

People were invited to share any other comments about the advance experience as they were so inclined. There were lots of laughs, some tears, many handshakes, hugs and thanks.

"Are there any other closing comments that you would like to share?" Just as the words escaped the Younger Facilitator's mouth, Beautiful stood, and with a determined, confident smile, began, "I have been struggling with a lack of inner beauty for much of my life. This advance has opened my eyes to believe that I am truly a beautiful person. From this moment forward, I will prepare through clarity of vision, practice by seeking out the multitude of tools I now have at my disposal, and live a life full of energy and passion. I will embrace each of life's experiences in the moment and seek the learning that each has to offer. I commit to fill my body, mind and spirit with positive affirmations that I am and will always be beautiful. As for others, I will help them discover the beauty in their own lives."

There was a moment of silence as everyone took in Beautiful's words. Freedom broke the silence by beginning a round of applause. As the clapping continued, Freedom stepped up and gave Beautiful a big bear hug. Beautiful felt a happiness she had not experienced in a long time. She felt beautiful.

Freedom, filled with gratitude said, "Wow, Beautiful. You are incredible! Thank you for your words. I have learned a lot from you. I have one other thing I want to share with the group. I came here as a Prisoner and I have made major strides toward being the Leader I know I can be. During the workshop, I had a conversation with the two facilitators. They asked me why I do what I do, and how I will know when I am successful. I could not answer at that moment and told the facilitators that I would think about it and answer them later. After pondering the question and thinking about all we have been learning here, I want to answer it now." He turned to face the two facilitators. "I do what I do now in my life out of necessity, commitments, responsibilities and habits. As the person I choose to become from this day forward, I do what I do because I choose to live passionately as a husband, father and a leader for God, others and myself. Happiness comes through positively embracing my challenges head-on. I define my success by learning and growing from each experience every day. I believe that in embracing the moment and living passionately, I find more happiness and freedom in my commitments and responsibilities. I will continually enjoy the practice of new positive habits in my life."

After a moment of contemplative silence, everyone respectfully applauded. Some of the women (Beautiful included), and even a couple of the men, stood up and gave Freedom hugs. Freedom was a little overwhelmed and tried holding back his tears, but they were evident to all.

Freedom thought, "Well, here I am, a macho man crying in front of all these people. And yet, I feel free. I am free!"

The train whistle blew, and the Younger Facilitator called all to standing in one last Ready Circle. Then he said, "I want to thank each and every one of you for this incredible opportunity. You have helped me grow and inspired me to continue to do what I love to do. Thank you so much. I want to thank your association director for his great leadership. And, of course, I thank my facilitating partner and lifelong friend, our Older Facilitator.

"Before I turn it over to our Older Facilitator, I would like to leave you with one final recommendation — and that is to go out into the world and *lie, cheat and steal*[118]."

Everyone stared in disbelief at the Younger Facilitator, wondering what he was saying. Then he continued. "Lie in bed at night and consider all the possibilities that life might bring. Cheat death by living life with passion every second of every minute of every day. And steal away five minutes from your hectic schedule to share an act of kindness with your fellow man."

There was a hush of silence as all pondered his words.

Then the Older Facilitator, standing in his strong stance, slowly looked around the circle, smiling at each person, and said, "I too want to thank you all for the opportunity to be with you, my peers as leaders, who are passionate about making a positive difference in this world of ours. I also want to thank your director for his leadership and inspiration in my life. And last, but certainly not least, I thank my friend and colleague, our Younger Facilitator, who puts such energy and inspiration into my life."

The Older Facilitator took a deep breath, let out a pleasant sigh, paused and then said, "We must bring closure to our learning experience. I suggest that we send off the phrase Seeking True North into the universe.

"Our world desperately needs strong positive leaders, so here is *the challenge*[119]: Go out and be strong leaders in your family, workplace and community. Be a person who strives for the lifelong mastery of living a balanced life in body, mind, spirit and relationships. In doing so, help others seek and achieve their own True North. Let's move close to the center of our circle."

They all moved closer into the center until they were shoulder to shoulder.

"Put your hands in the center, and when I say the word Passion we will all lift our hands and shout 'Seeking True North.' Ready? Preparation, Practice, Passion!"

With that, they all raised their hands and shouted, "SEEKING TRUE NORTH!"

Epilogue

Two years later at the alumni "Renewal" retreat — that is, "advance" — Freedom and Beautiful sat on a bench overlooking the mountains, which appeared incredibly peaceful that evening.

"Hard to believe two years have gone by since we were all here," Freedom said as he gazed toward the setting sun over the trails they had hiked.

"I know," replied Beautiful.

"So how are you, Beautiful?" asked Freedom.

"Well, you know from our e-mails and phone conversations that a lot has happened in the past two years. I can hardly believe how much better my life has been. My husband and I are like two people madly in love. We hold hands while walking down the street or at the mall. We went on a second honeymoon a few months ago. It's just incredible. My daughter is doing better in school. I think it may be because I am more relaxed, confident and able to help her. I constantly use the tools we learned. Preparation, practice and passion have become continuous thoughts and actions in my life. Some of my favorite tools are the anchors, goals action planning, rapport-building skills and Virtual Reality Vision Board. I am on a constant quest to find new tools and apply them in my life. And my performance at work is off the charts. I received my second raise, and bonus checks are a regular now. And what is weird about it is that I used to sometimes feel tired or depressed, but now I feel consistently energized and quite passionate about my life and work! Of course, there are problems, but they get solved. The greater thing for me is that I feel confident in myself, and know, beyond doubt, that I am a beautiful person."

They looked at each other and smiled.

"How about you, Freedom? How are you?"

Freedom turned to look at the mountains and sighed with pleasure. "Wonderful. I feel so free in my life! I continually prepare for my desired results, I practice and create passion, and I embrace the process as I accomplish my desired outcomes. I continue to discover new meaning and purpose in my life. It is amazing. The Seeking True North experience has caused me to be so focused in life. My marriage has improved, also. My wife and I are really enjoying being together and watching the kids grow up into great human beings. Work is much better. I have been able to confidently lead, manage and speak up when I feel I have something of value to share. One of the greatest growth areas for me has been sharing the concepts that I have learned so that others can grow and benefit in their lives. I still have tough days and struggles, but I am passionate about continually improving my abilities and helping others to grow in their lives. My income has increased also; that has enabled us to invest more, which we'd wanted to do but couldn't in the past. Instead of waiting, whining and hoping for miracles, I have become a miracle maker for others and myself. I have been able to focus on embracing each moment, and that has made all the difference.

"Some of my favorite tools are the visual, auditory and kinesthetic communication styles, the thumb-check assessment for a quick management check, the personal motto and the speaking stance. Every week, I practice by glancing through my list of tools, updating my list and adding new tools I learn from various sources. That is helpful to keep things fresh in my mind. Despite the daily challenges at work and at home, my life has definitely changed for the better. But most importantly, I know that I am free to be who I feel I should be in this life, and I am willing to live for it and die for it."

They spent several hours sharing with each other, talking about how they had explored the search for True North with family, friends and co-workers. Beautiful confided that she had even started a Seeking True North group back home that met once a month to discuss and share new tools with each other. She finished by saying, "We even had a Seeking True North party at the New Year and shared our commitment to growth, the tools we are using and the challenges we are facing along the way. We are each on a lifelong quest to find True North and help others do the same."

* * *

Freedom and Beautiful remained lifelong friends. Little did they know that, in the years ahead, they would be put to a life-threatening test that demanded all the skills they had learned together and forced them to learn many more. Every few years, they and their families got together for a vacation somewhere nice and enjoyed a slice of life together. And, of course, they each carried their *compass*[120] always.

Part I Summary

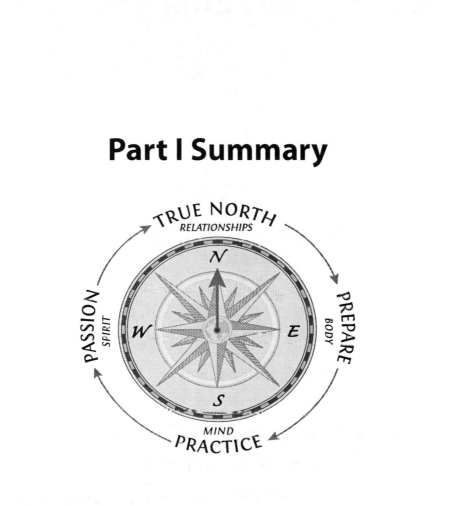

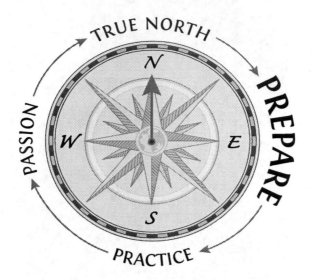

It Is Very Simple to Prepare:

1. **Choose what you want to be prepared for...**

   ...and determine your desired end results.

2. **Write out your clearly defined desired end results...**

   ...including a date by which you will achieve them.

3. **Expect that you will achieve your desired end results...**

   ...results full of purpose and meaning.

It Is Very Simple to Practice:

1. **Seek out and choose...**

   ... the Model, Method or Tool you desire to utilize.

2. **Force yourself into the Growth Zone**

   ... and take consistent action.

3. **Seek feedback and focus on the process...**

   ... as you adapt your strategy to achieve your desired end results.

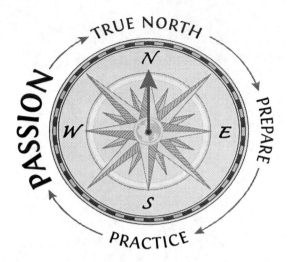

It Is Very Simple to Create Passion:

1. **Make a conscious decision to embrace the moment...**

   ...and create happiness and meaning in your life.

2. **Surround yourself with positive people...**

   ...to learn from the meaning of each experience.

3. **Feed your body, mind and spirit...**

   ...with positive, healthy food, and embrace the process with every step along your path.

PART II
Models, Methods, Tools and Habits

We need many tools to help us in Seeking True North in our lives. All of the models, methods, tools and habits mentioned in the story of *Seeking True North* are described in this section. From these, you can choose specific ones to prepare, practice and be passionate about to cultivate your life and relationships, as well as a healthier body, mind and spirit. It is up to you to grow, learn and assist others in their growth.

Access www.SeekingTrueNorth.com to discover how others are using the tools described in this book. In addition, we have also added new models, methods and tools as well as an interactive discussion board for continuous growth and development.

Index of Models, Methods, Tools and Habits

Glossary of Models, Methods, Tools and Habits

1. MASTERY MOUNTAIN

Living our lives to our truest potential involves continually learning new things. The following model presents a progression that we all experience as we become aware of, learn and ultimately master any concept. This model applies not only to leadership, but to every part of our lives. Formally, it provides a structure for understanding and developing competencies. A *competency* can be defined as a personal trait or set of habits leading to more effective or superior performance. There are four stages to developing any competency.

» *Unconscious incompetence* is the stage where a person is simply unaware that a subject, idea, perspective or skill exists. You aren't even aware that you should know or do something differently.

» *Conscious incompetence* is the stage where a person becomes aware that there is a different, and often better, way to do something. You become aware that you need to be doing something differently, but you're not sure how and don't have the skill.

» *Conscious competence* is the stage where a person is capable of performing whatever concept or skill they are doing. At this stage, it does require some thought and conscious effort to perform.

» *Unconscious competence* is the stage where a person achieves the level of expert and can apply knowledge, use skills and respond to a situation instantly without thinking about it. The person understands what needs to be done and does it without even thinking about it.

This model is a natural part of life. How do you turn decades into days? Learn from those that already have qualities and characteristics that you desire. Once we master a new skill, it is natural to continually challenge ourselves and thus come right back down to unconscious incompetence. In management, this is known as the Peter Principle, where you get promoted to your level of incompetence.

Confidence Development. This model contains stages parallel to those in the competency model: *unconscious self-doubt, conscious self-doubt, conscious confidence* and *unconscious confidence.* It is vital to build confidence along with competence. Continually build your confidence by celebrating and being proud of the things you do well. Embrace failure as a learning opportunity that propels you into future growth. As your confidence grows, so will your ability to achieve your desired end results.

Life is a repetitive climbing of both Confidence and Competence Mountains to ascend Mastery Mountain.

2. PRISONER, VACATIONER OR LEADER

People take on three types of attitudes as they approach life. We will find ourselves in at least one of these three modes in our thinking and actions every day. *Prisoners* are close-minded and often attempt to draw down those around them. *Vacationers* show up for an experience, yet are rarely proactive; they do not truly seek value from an experience. *Leaders* continually seek out value in any experience, even those that involve a failure. Leaders also maintain a positive attitude and facilitate the growth and development of others. The choice is ours to make. Choose to be a leader in life.

3. ADVANCE

Become aware of the language that people use and the subconscious meanings attached to words. Consider modifying your language and renaming certain things to support your desired outcomes. In this instance, we took the word *retreat* and replaced it with advance; the latter's meaning of "forward momentum" creates positive associations for any group we are working with.

4. WHEN THE STUDENT IS READY, THE TEACHER APPEARS

As you seek continuous growth in your life, train your mind to consciously and subconsciously become aware of, and alert for, opportunities. This first involves being open to the idea that what you see, hear or experience could be an opportunity to learn or grow in some regard. It is when you are continuously "ready" that the teacher appears.

5. FORMING JUDGMENTS AND ASSUMPTIONS

Understanding the process of creating assumptions is one of the most powerful forms of awareness that one can embrace. One classic model for understanding this process is called the Ladder of Inference, developed by Chris Argyris. Argyris describes the progressive process of making observations, gathering information, making assumptions and deciding on action as being similar to climbing up a "ladder of inference."

This model shows how we create assumptions by selecting data based on belief systems that we have developed over time. The critical aspect of this model is to understand the basis of our assumptions and to be aware that we continually select data to reinforce our belief systems. As you consider the judgments and assumptions that you make, first consider your belief systems and how they filter the information that you select.

6. MAKING EYE CONTACT

It is important to make eye contact with people during your communication with them. In American culture, we typically want to match the degree and frequency of eye contact to that being made by the person you are speaking with. When you are addressing a small group or team, scan the audience and make eye contact with as many people as possible. This is a simple yet powerful communication technique.

7. THE MOST IMPORTANT QUESTION

"What is most important to me in my_____?" We have termed this "The Most Important Question" because it seeks to clarify what is most important to an individual in a particular area of life. This is a value-based question in which the blank spot is filled in with the value you are seeking to understand or clarify. For example, if you want to find out what is most important to someone in his or her relationships, you would insert the word "relationships" into the blank. Use this question whenever you want to get to the core of what is most important to another individual.

8. MAGIC STATEMENT

"Why was this experience the 'best?'" The Magic Statement is a tool for visualizing your intended outcome. The process involves individuals answering the question and thus creating and articulating their desired end results before experiencing them. As in the Pygmalion effect, this method allows you not only to live your future but also to create it. The Magic Statement can be used as a team process whereby participants in a group share with each other what will make for an outstanding experience from their individual perspectives. This serves to create a shared situational awareness, in which each individual gains an understanding of what will make for a successful experience.

9. LOOKS, SOUNDS AND FEELS

It's a fact: According to the science of neurolinguistics, humans use three typical communication styles. We communicate predominantly through:

» Visual means (what we see through our eyes or in our minds);
» Auditory means (words and dialogue with others or ourselves); and
» Kinesthetic means (how we feel about things internally or how things actually feel externally).

When presenting, teaching or communicating to groups, it is important to incorporate all three styles so that you connect with each person.

10. GIVE YOUR NAME

It is important to have people become familiar with each others' names at the beginning of a shared group experience. There are many pneumonic devices, activities and initiatives designed for this purpose. One very simple one is to repeat the names of the participants as often as possible in the beginning of a shared experience.

11. WHY TOOL

Asking ourselves, "Why do I want to achieve this or do that?" is important in understanding the reason or motivation behind our desired end result. As we remain stalwart through many challenges and failures on our journey toward True North, our purpose will drive us to persist and to advance again and again toward our goals and desired end results. Create a very powerful "why" and continually associate it with your outcomes.

12. RECITE IT TO YOURSELF OFTEN

The act of reciting or reading aloud your purpose for wanting to achieve major goals in life is a powerful vehicle in bringing your desired end results to fruition. When you have a strong enough *why*, you will figure out a *way*.

13. PERSONAL JOURNAL

Keeping a journal is a powerful way to record your progress and to organize and explore your thoughts over a specific time frame. The act of reflecting and writing down your thoughts takes your learning to a deeper level. This allows you to integrate and apply your life experiences toward a positive future. When you have written down important goals in your journal, it's a beautiful thing to go back later and realize that you have achieved them. Your journal can be as simple as a pocket-sized notebook or as complex as a Franklin Planner. Some people have little interest in using a journal. Seek ways to make the process of writing a journal fun and relevant to your specific interests and lifestyle.

14. WRITING WHAT YOU THINK

As you read this or any book, or listen to someone speak, be sure to write down *your* ideas about what *you* want to accomplish and how you will accomplish your desired outcomes. This will allow you to assimilate the information you gain as it applies to your life.

15. 100 GOALS

Those who write down their goals are more likely to achieve them. Create a powerful tool in achieving your goals by writing in a journal or composition book at least 100 goals and desires you would like to achieve. The time frame can be short, medium or long-term; you can even create a 100-year goals list for your lifetime. Goals can be simple and small, such as saving for a new bicycle, wanting to go to the beach with the children, or saving money for a new watch. They can be things desired in the future, such as a particular type of home or camp or an adventurous vacation. Or they can be something huge, like owning a successful business, earning a million dollars, ceasing to smoke, or losing 150 pounds and staying healthy for life!

The process of *thinking* about and writing your goals and desires is a powerful vehicle for bringing about positive change. When used in conjunction with the SMART (Specific, Measurable, Action-Oriented, Realistic and Timely) goal system, this process creates a powerful method for achieving specific results.

16. ROUND OF APPLAUSE

Take time to recognize progress by applauding people. Applause creates positive motion and sound within a group of people. Keep in mind that there are many types of applause. Be creative!

17. TAKE YOUR FINGER AND POINT

In a group setting, the leader points to a specific person and has the group acknowledge that person through some positive statement. The pointing provides a powerful kinesthetic experience for the individual being praised; it also breaks negative connotations generally associated with pointing at someone.

18. POKE YOURSELF

Poke yourself and reinforce a positive affirmation. It is very simple and creates positive energy within you and within the group. This is a quick energizer that can be used with anyone, at any point. This works well when all the people in a group are saying the same thing at the same time.

19. STORY OF THE RIGHT ADVANCE

In this activity, each person is secretly assigned to observe another, to catch them doing positive or "right" things throughout a shared experience. To determine who observes whom, have participants write their names on cards and then stand in a circle. Next, improvise a story using the words "left" and "right" as often as possible. For example…

*"This is the story about the **right** advance. Leaders **left** one day in a relative way to discover the **right** ways to …"*

Each time participants hear the words "left" and "right," they will pass their cards in that direction. When the story is over, participants will secretly observe the person whose card they have.

This activity serves to create a culture in which all participants are focused on adding value and watching others do the same.

20. THE GIFT

This activity is a simple but powerful way to reinforce learning and sharing. Each person in the group purchases a theme-based gift (within a set cost limit) and is secretly assigned another person to give the gift to. The gift is shared at the conclusion of the advance. Typically, this activity is linked with the Right Advance activity so that each participant gives the gift to the person being observed and shares positive observations about the person at the same time as giving the gift.

21. MENTORS

Our friend, Dr. Charlie "Tremendous" Jones, tells us that his best mentors have been people he has read about in books. Do your homework and choose a few books to study as well as a few people to hang out with (and give to). Then learn from those mentors. Continue the lifelong process of choosing the particular character traits you want to learn from people, books, films and other sources.

22. THE HIGHEST ORDER OF LEARNING

The highest order of learning is when you teach someone to teach someone else. When we achieve this, our lessons in life become transferable, allowing multiple people to benefit. Learning how to learn and teach is a lifelong pursuit that will continually expand our effectiveness as human beings.

23. CORE VALUES

Recognizing, analyzing and aligning our core values and beliefs are vital to effective living. Our decisions in life are based on our core values, values that we hold in our conscious and subconscious mind. Often, we form beliefs based on assumptions that may not promote a happy and fulfilled life. Examine your core values and beliefs, and list the rules and beliefs that guide your decisions in life. Consider how each belief affects your daily and long-term actions. Then adjust your values and beliefs on paper and put them in a healthier sequence. The goal is to have healthy, positive guidelines for your behavior that will lead you through a fulfilled life. Monitor the effect of your alignment over several months of practice.

24. PYGMALION EFFECT

Also known as the "teacher-expectancy effect," this refers to situations in which students perform better than other students simply because they are expected to do so. This is also known as the self-fulfilling prophecy. You can apply this principle to yourself by expecting success. And when you expressly expect others to do great things, it helps them to achieve them.

25. PERSONAL MOTTO

Create a personal motto for yourself — a few sentences describing the "you" that you most want to be. Describe yourself the way you want to be no matter what happens on any given day. Describe yourself the way you want to be despite past performance or others' opinions of you. Rehearse your motto every day.

26. COMMANDER, PARTNER AND FACILITATOR LEADERSHIP STYLES

There are many models for leadership. One of our favorites describes three leadership styles. The Commander takes charge on an as-needed basis. The Partner leads by joining forces and decision-making within the group. The Facilitator leads by asking questions and inspiring the group to function on their own. Your goal should be to become a master at shifting among these three styles as needed every day.

27. SETTING GROUP VALUES

In this process, the group sets core values for being together. Led by the facilitator, the group discusses the most vital part of team synergy and sets guidelines for behavior. The facilitator asks questions such as:

» How do you want to be treated while you are together as a group today? During your project? For the duration of your time together?

» How do you want to treat others?

» What are the qualities of the environment you would like to have while together?

» What values are particularly important to you as an individual that you would like to promote in this team?

As people share this information, the facilitator records it on a flip chart, paper or notepad. The group then establishes ownership of these core values as an objective measure of team behavior. Ideally, the group should decide to adhere to the values through mutual consensus. In certain instances, the team leader sets the group values. These values can be referred to at any time throughout the shared experience.

28. THUMB-CHECK ASSESSMENT

"Thumbs" voting is a consensus-building tool that provides a process for a team to vote on a particular proposal. Someone voices a proposal, and the group takes a quick vote on it with the Thumb Check. Once established, this tool can greatly enhance efficiency for coming to consensus quickly.

» Thumbs up: "I am in 100 percent. Let's move forward."

» Thumbs sideways: "I am in. I don't necessarily fully agree, but I will support the decision of the group." You may or may not want to take comments about the decision.

> »   Thumb down: "I have a concern that needs to be addressed."

29. EMOTIONAL INTELLIGENCE ASSESSMENT

As effective human beings, we must continually cultivate our emotional intelligence. There is a large and growing body of research describing the "soft skills" or "street smarts" known as emotional intelligence.

Below are brief descriptions of 15 areas in which we can grow, as developed and described by Dr. Reuven BarOn. Each description is accompanied by a related affirmation. It is up to you to create more affirmations, form stronger beliefs and values for yourself, and take action to grow in each of these competencies. At some point in your developmental process, we recommend you take the BarOn EQ-i assessment to measure your competencies. This will give you a powerful tool to monitor your progress as you seek to grow in specific areas of your life.

Intrapersonal

> »   Self-Regard: The ability to understand, respect and accept yourself.
> »   Affirmation: I understand, accept and respect myself.
> »   Emotional Self-Awareness: The ability to know what you feel and why.
> »   Affirmation: I know what I feel and why.
> »   Assertiveness: The ability to express your thoughts and feelings, ask for what you need and defend your rights in a constructive manner.
> »   Affirmation: I am able to express my thoughts and feelings and ask for what I need. I defend my rights in a constructive manner.

» Independence: Your ability to be self-reliant and autonomous in thoughts and actions.

» Affirmations: I am self-reliant and autonomous in my thoughts and actions.

» Self-Actualization: Qualities that enable you to fulfill your potential and create an interesting, exciting and meaningful life.

» Affirmation: I achieve my potential and get involved in things that lead to an interesting, exciting and meaningful life.

Interpersonal

» Empathy: The ability to be sensitive to what, how and why people feel and think the way they do — to care about others and show interest and concern for them.

» Affirmation: I am sensitive to what, how and why people feel and think the way they do. I care about others and show interest and concern for them.

» Social responsibility: The ability to be a responsible, cooperative and contributing member of society — being socially conscious and concerned about others.

» Affirmation: I am a responsible, cooperative and contributing member of society. I am socially conscious and concerned for others.

» Interpersonal Relationship: The ability to establish and maintain mutually satisfying relationships and be comfortable in giving and receiving affection.

» Affirmation: I establish and maintain mutually satisfying relationships. I am comfortable giving and receiving affection.

Stress Management

» Stress Tolerance: The ability to actively and positively deal with stressful situations.

» Affirmation: I withstand stressful situations by actively and positively coping with stress.

» Impulse Control: The ability to resist or delay an impulse, drive or temptation.

» Affirmation: I resist or delay an impulse, drive or temptation when I choose.

Adaptability

» Reality Testing: The ability to objectively see, hear and feel details of a situation.

» Affirmation: I sense and tune into the immediate situation and can see things objectively — the way they are, rather than how I wish or fear them to be.

» Flexibility: The ability to adjust feelings, thoughts and behaviors to changing situations and conditions; being open to different ideas and ways of doing things.

» Affirmation: I adjust my feelings, thoughts and behaviors to changing situations and conditions. I am open to different ideas and ways of doing things.

» Problem Solving: The ability to identify problems and to generate and implement solutions.

» Affirmations: I identify problems as well as generate and implement solutions.

General Mood

» Optimism: The ability to maintain a positive attitude and view of life even when times are tough.

» Affirmation: I look at the brighter side of life and maintain a positive attitude even when times are tough.

» Happiness: The ability to feel good, to relax and to be at ease in situations.

» Affirmation: I feel good and at ease in both work and leisure situations. I relax and enjoy my life.

30. INTERACTIVE CARD GAME

Take any information that you desire to teach, and express its elements on small cards. Then use the cards as a means of exploring the information in a group setting. For example, use cards containing the names and definitions of the 15 emotional intelligence competencies to explore those competencies with the group.

31. AFFIRMATIONS

Webster's Dictionary defines affirmation as "a positive assertion; to assert as valid or confirmed; to express dedication to; a solemn declaration."

Affirmations are written in the active, present tense as positive statements. For example, if you are creating an affirmation for yourself in the area of self-esteem, you might write, "Every day, I do something to better myself as a great person." Avoid using statements written in future tense, such as, "I will become a better person," or "I will quit smoking." For something like quitting smoking, it is much more powerful to write, "I put into my body only what is healthy for me." Avoid negatively referenced statements such as, "I don't eat sweets." This is because, when saying this to yourself, you are visualizing the possibility of that negative thing. It is much more powerful to write in the positive mode something like, "I eat only what is best for me," or "Every day, I eat healthy foods that produce a healthy body for me." Writing positive affirmations and rehearsing them should be a constant, lifelong process to specifically program your thinking to match your desired end results.

32. DIVIDE GROUP INTO FOUR QUADRANTS

There are endless methods of dividing groups into smaller groups. The "Wolf" story is one of our favorites. Favorite colors, seasons, vacation locations and beverages are alternative ways of doing so.

33. EXPECTATIONS QUADRANT MODEL

This model developed by Inscape Publishing provides a framework for exploring expectations across a quadrant whose axes are *met* and *unmet, spoken* and *unspoken*. Addressing unmet, unspoken expectations can constructively reduce conflict and frustration in the workplace. In the pursuit of True North as we climb Mastery Mountain, we must seek for our expectations to be spoken and met.

	MET	**UNMET**
S P O K E N		
U N S P O K E N		

34. MEMORIZE NAMES

There is no such thing as a bad memory. You have either a trained or untrained memory; the choice is yours. There are many pneumonic devices to increase your memory power. Attaching silly associations to people's names will creatively stimulate your brain to remember them.

35. HAND OF REASON

If as facilitator or leader you wish to gain the attention of a group or to quiet it quickly, teach participants the Hand of Reason. When participants see you raise your hand in the air, each person immediately raises his or her hand and stops talking. It is important to introduce this tool to the group, have all present agree to use the tool, and practice it a few times. Make sure that you have the commitment of each person to respect and use this tool before you implement it.

36. HOW DO YOU MEAN?

"How do you mean?" This question is a powerful technique that can be used to diffuse frustration, foster effective communication, build rapport and deepen understanding. Over the years, many of us have developed a negative association with the question "What do you mean?" and often react negatively or defensively to it. By asking, "How do you mean?" instead, we express interest, rather than impatience or confusion, and convey our true desire to understand.

37. TRAIN WHISTLE

Use a variety of fun noises to call people to attention: whistles, drums or, of course, "more cow-bell!" Another method is the Listening Links, in which you link arms with another person and stop talking until everyone is linked with someone else and all stop talking.

38. CONTINUUM

This exercise facilitates interactive discussion around a particular topic. Simply provide a topic and have participants form a line, positioning themselves where they believe they are on a continuum relative to that topic. This is typically completed without talking. For example, you might ask participants to stand closer to one end of the line if they are very confident in their ability to lead their current team, and to stand toward the other end of the line if they are not. The continuum quickly mixes participants of various abilities and comfort levels around a given topic.

39. WANDER AROUND AND CONNECT

Make time to engage and meet with people. While you interact with others, practice using your visual, auditory and kinesthetic (VAK) communication styles to build rapport. You will get more of what you want by constantly becoming better at your relationship skills.

40. READY CIRCLE

The Ready Circle is a group-processing formation where everyone can see the eyes of everyone else while standing in a circle. This is based on the fundamental understanding that effective communication involves much more than verbal modality. Body language and eye contact are keys to understanding the full meaning of what individuals are communicating in a group setting. When you are ready for a group discussion, have people gather in a Ready Circle.

41. ZONING IN MODEL

Zoning in requires that we consider how we are living our lives. Humans have a natural tendency to stay in the comfort zone and do the same things day in and day out. As we seek personal and professional growth, we must continually challenge ourselves to step out of that comfort zone and engage in activities that are challenging to us. Living in the growth zone allows us to expand our capacity as human beings. Zoning In is the process of becoming aware of where you are now, and of recognizing and embracing the value of engaging in challenging pursuits in life.

42. PRACTICE FOR 12 MONTHS

Committing to a growth process of practicing a particular skill or competency for at least 12 consecutive months is essential. As the saying goes, "repetition is the mother of skill." Practicing for 12 months will enable you to measure your success as you grow.

43. SENSORY ACUITY

Developing sensory acuity is the process of increasing your awareness by observing what is and is not working in your life and making appropriate adjustments. There are formal mechanisms of feedback that can facilitate this growth and development. These include reflecting on your own performance, analyzing the results of the task you perform and seeking feedback from others.

44. SEEK THE OPINION OF OTHERS

Surround yourself with a few people you can trust to give you honest, candid feedback about who you are and how you perform. We recommend occasionally taking a 360-degree assessment where your peers, subordinates and boss have the opportunity to share feedback on attitude, competencies and so on.

One of the most important words in the English language is "ask." We do not get what we do not ask for, and that includes feedback about our growth and development.

45. STORYTELLING

Storytelling is the oldest means of teaching on planet Earth. We all should have at least two or three powerful stories memorized and ready to tell. Join your local storytelling or Toastmasters club to hone this skill.

46. PSYCHOLOGICAL ANCHORS AND TRIGGERS

An anchor or trigger is anything that comes into our perception, consciously or subconsciously, that has an impact on our emotional state. As human beings, we use anchors or triggers, at both levels, all day, every day. In brief, anchors involve any of the five senses — sight, smell, touch, taste and hearing — as they relate to the ego, id, superego and spirit. As they relate to anchors, these senses can be incorporated into the three main communication styles: visual, auditory and kinesthetic. Anchors are very powerful mechanisms that affect our emotional states. Having an awareness of, and knowing how to use, these anchors are important skills in communication, influence, personal health and empowerment.

47. EDIFY ANOTHER

Showing appreciation of another person by complimenting or "edifying" them is a powerful tool. Remember that the purpose of such praise is to build up the other person, not you. Honest appreciation backed up by facts boosts the receiving person's morale, spirit and ability; for the person giving the compliment, it is a great way to be a positive influence in the lives of others. Make giving genuine compliments part of your "norm" in life.

48. PASSION MOUNTAIN MODEL

This model is used to describe four levels of passion: Passion Dreamer, Passion Day Hiker, Passion Momentum and Pure Passion. Each level indicates various intensities and can be used to evaluate your passion in a particular area.

49. PATHWAY

This exercise is designed to explore and document major emotional landmarks, breakthroughs and significant events in your life. This process creates a powerful form of disclosure and bonding among team members. There are many methods for facilitating this powerful leadership and team building process.

50. REFLECTION

Also known as processing or debriefing, the reflection process is used to determine the value of any learning experience. After engaging in developmental activities and initiatives, take some time to process the significance and relevance of the activity. Many frameworks can be used in the reflection process. These all revolve around analyzing the individual and team experience and how those experiences apply to personal and professional lives. It is critical to consider the action plans that can be implemented as a result of the reflection, and to document your ideas and plans.

51. EMBRACING THE NOW

Embracing the Now means that you are fully awake to the present moment. In this state of being, we are filled with neither worry for the future nor regret of the past. It is in this state that passion lives. Make a choice to be fully present and allow yourself to just "be."

52. PRAX FACTOR

The Prax Factor is a tool for consciously choosing the people with whom we spend our time. Life is too short to be surrounded with people who don't support us or provide the energy and passion for living life to its fullest. Make a list of the qualities you want to have in those around you and continually seek out those people who have the characteristics and qualities that you want in your life. Soon enough, those qualities will be integrated into your system, helping you to live the life that you desire.

53. REFRAME THE MEANING

We have the power to attach meaning to every experience in our lives. Most of us do this sub-consciously every day. The goal of this tool is to master the skill of consciously creating the meaning you choose for the experiences in your life. Use this tool when it is difficult to discover the meaning of an experience. Also, if you see an experience as negative or non-beneficial at the beginning, ask yourself and those around you, "How can I look at this differently?" or "What could be positive about this experience?" Talk with others about how that experience could be a beneficial one. Continually train your mind to seek out the positive aspects of any situation. This is critical to creating and maintaining happiness and passion in your life. Remember this saying: "The only bad experience is the one not learned from."

54. "I ENVISION" BOOKLET

An "I Envision" booklet allows you to create and record the details of all you expect to have happen in a specific event or circumstance in your life. That's it! That's all there is to this simple but powerful tool. Make one yourself!

55. CONDITIONING PROGRAM

Maintaining a healthy body is a cornerstone to living a life full of passion and energy. Utilize the resources around you to create and maintain your ideal conditioning program. Setting a series of goals for yourself and having partners to keep you on track will facilitate your process. Along the way, remember that the best exercise program is the one that you do!

56. NUTRITION

There are thousands of ways to consider the best nutrition for your body. Very simply, put into your body only what is best for you! Two important concepts to practice are reducing your overall sugar intake and taking in alkalizing instead of acidifying foods and beverages.

57. HYDRATION

We all know that water is good for you; it is the one of the most abundant resources on the earth and in our bodies. Drinking water can help boost energy while helping to reduce problems such as back pain. Make hydration a consistent part of daily living...DRINK UP!

58. MENTAL IMAGING

Star performers in every area of life use this technique on a regular basis. Professional athletes, martial artists, rock climbers, public speakers and business executives all use mental imaging to visualize achieving their desired end results. When you use this technique, visualize achieving the results that are most important to you. Create vivid mental pictures, with the motion, color, brightness, sights, sounds, smells, textures and feelings that you desire before you experience them.

59. VIRTUAL REALITY VISION BOARD

Create a picture collage for yourself based on what you want your future to be. Overlay pictures of you in action on scenes of your desired future. Place your Virtual Reality Vision Board in a prominent place and look at it often, imagining that you have already accomplished your goals.

60. PRAYER OF JABEZ

There are many books written about prayer and meditation. We recommend that you choose a few methods from each and begin to create the healthy balance among body, mind, spirit and in your relationships by preparing, practicing and becoming more passionate through the vehicle of prayer and meditation. The *Prayer of Jabez* is one such book.

61. ASK

Ask, and you shall receive. Being able to ask for what you need and desire is a very important skill. Break through the fear of being ignorant and reduce your time spent learning by asking others for what you need! As your success builds, your results create positive benefits for others that have helped you along your pathway to finding True North.

62. SUPPORT TEAM

Create a support team of people you can count on to give you honest, candid feedback. They should also be those who have your best interests in mind and help you see learning opportunities as positive experiences. Select your team carefully and let them know that they are on it and how you expect them to help you. And, of course, let them know how you can help them in return!

63. MODEL AFTER OTHERS' SUCCESS

The formula is simple. Find someone who is achieving the results you desire, and find out what they are doing to achieve those results. When you take another person's actions with the same syntax (formula) and apply them to your life, then you will produce very nearly the same results. Choose people to model yourself after. However, be careful to maintain your own unique identity and creativity. The world will benefit from your positive creations!

64. WHEEL OF LIFE

The wheel of life is a preparation process intended to clarify the roles that you desire to constantly focus on in your life. Write out a detailed vision for the personal and professional roles in your life. Then create goals in each of these areas to measure your focus and improvement.

65. KICK-BUTT PRINCIPLE

Let's face it: We are going to have many failures throughout our lifetimes. And when we do, it can be hard to get back into action. The Kick-butt Principle is there to get you going again! Don't let failure get you down. And have friends around who will always keep you kicking butt!

66. WORD SEND

Gather your group together in a circle and choose a word or phrase that represents a shared experience. Then send it off into the universe with a shout or a whisper. This is an excellent method for achieving closure to a learning experience. Remember that all things begin with a thought or word.

67. CARPE MOMENTO!

This is similar to *carpe diem*, but focused on the immediate present. Translated, it means, "Seize the moment!"

68. THE MOST INCREDIBLY AWESOME DAY

This is simply a belief statement that I, Erick Erickson, use every morning upon waking. I say to myself, "Today is one of the most incredibly awesome days of my entire life!" And guess what? Most often, it turns out just that way!

69. BREATHWALK

This is a powerful energizer and health and wellness tool that can be used alone or with a group. The Breathwalk is composed of three interconnected elements: Specific walking patterns, combined with specific breathing patterns, used with specific directed thought. The four-four pattern is the most basic to begin with. As you walk, take four sharp breaths in through the nasal cavity, then expel four sharp breaths out through the nasal cavity, matching your breathing with each step you take. After you continue this process for several minutes, you will notice a significant increase in your perceptual awareness of the world around you and a change in your emotional and physical state. A significant amount of research has been done on the efficacy and wellness benefits of the Breathwalk. When you do this with another person, match your breathing, steps, arm movement and body position to increase the rapport between you.

70. MACRO AND MICRO STRETCHES

With the group in a Ready Circle, one person starts with a macro stretch such as jumping jacks, which involves full-body movements or major muscle parts. Then, around the circle, each person does jumping jacks until it comes back around to the leader. As all continue to do jumping jacks, the next person starts a micro stretch (involving small body parts or movements) such as finger stretches. The finger stretching goes around the circle and back to the one who started the finger stretch. The next person switches back to a macro stretch, and the fun continues!

71. LAUGHTER STRETCH

In a Ready Circle, a leader starts with a giggle and progresses to a chuckle. The group matches it. Next comes a bit of laughter, and the group follows suit. Good, loud laughing is introduced now as the group really gets into the hilarious stretch of the mind, body and spirit. The activity finishes with all-out hysterical, knee-slapping, eye-watering peals of laughter. Get ready for a very unique and rewarding experience with this one.

72. MEDITATION

This skill should be used by everyone for the daily calming of the mind, soul, body and spirit. Much of the simple power of meditation has been lost in Western culture over the centuries. Commit to learning a few basic meditation skills and add them to your daily health and wellness routine. You can meditate in a traditional silent mode while practicing yoga, walking or sitting.

73. MEANING OF THIS DAY

A healthy habit is to determine the meaning of your day each morning upon waking. You determine the meaning, which can be different each day. This can go along with the meaning of each day being "the most incredibly awesome day of your entire life!"

74. TO INFINITY AND BEYOND

A well-timed, resounding tribute to *Toy Story's* Buzz Lightyear is a simple group affirmation to keep thinking in a fun, positive spirit.

75. FUN FACTS

Print out interesting facts about your area and have them ready to pass out to your group. Have the participants create questions and quiz each other about their knowledge. Give a moment for people to answer. If no one knows, then read the answer.

76. INFORMATION CARDS

Information from a specific book that the entire group has read is printed on cards. Each person receives a card with a different tidbit of information. Have participants pair up and share information with each other about how the book has influenced them, based on the information on their respective cards. This can be extended into a public-speaking practice session as people share their learning with the whole group.

77. CREATE A SYSTEM

There are many ways of exploring systems. These can be something as simple as an orderly, effective means of ensuring that all in the group have a lunch (as in the story in Part One) or as complex as business systems models that analyze return on investment (ROI). When working with groups, one key focus is on the analysis of the process of how the system is created and implemented.

78. SPEAKING STANCE

As a speaker, facilitator or presenter, your initial delivery should begin with a firm speaking stance. For the first few moments of your presentation, imagine that you are like a tree with roots growing into the floor and you cannot move. After that initial firm beginning, you can begin to move your body in sync with your presentation.

79. TOASTMASTERS

Join your local Toastmasters public speaking club. Such clubs are located across the United States as well as internationally. The ability to communicate and articulate well in public is a skill that all successful people must seek to master. Simply take the time to practice what you want to effectively communicate while walking down the street, in your home or anywhere you feel comfortable. Join your local public speaking club, take some courses and get out and practice!

80. MANDATORY BOOK READING AND CD LISTENING

We encourage every business and organization to set up mandatory quarterly reading and CD listening. Choose booklets that are short, sweet and powerful, so people can absorb the same language and thinking. This, done consistently, will infuse synergized mindsets, beliefs and actions into any organization.

81. I CAN'T BELIEVE . . .

This chant is a way to celebrate being in an amazing place with amazing people. Start by having participants point their fingers up in the air. Then have them poke the shoulder of the person to their right. While they are poking, raise your voice with enthusiasm and have the entire group repeat after you:

"I can't believe

that I am

at this team advance [or at your location]

with a leader like you!

[Say the last sentence with real oomph!]

You are incredible!"

This short activity can also be used to compliment one particular person in the group. You can have everyone point to that person and repeat a complimentary phrase.

82. SELF TALK

Always be mindful of your internal dialogue. Negative, self-limiting talk should be erased from your mind and thoughts. When you catch yourself entertaining such thoughts, stop, refocus and re-channel your thoughts in a positive direction. We must feed our minds with positive data if we want positive things to come out! You can do this proactively by creating affirmations, statements and beliefs about who you desire to be and say these to yourself often.

83. BECOME A WITNESS

The practice of becoming a witness involves stepping outside of yourself and observing your thoughts as a third party. As you pay attention to those conversations in your mind, determine whether the thoughts you are "hearing" are beneficial to a peaceful, productive state of mind. As a witness to your mind, you increase your awareness of thoughts and begin creating positive patterns.

84. DOING FANTASTICALLY — AND GETTING BETTER

This tool is simply a positive attitude builder. When someone asks you, "How are you today?" respond with, "I am doing fantastically, but you know what?" Pause for a few seconds until the person asks, "What?" Then you finish with "Getting better!" Say this to yourself often enough and you actually will feel fantastic and keep getting better, every day.

85. BACKWARDS SHOPPING

For a lesson in paradigm shifts, go grocery shopping backwards by pushing the cart from the front end. It is a wild experience guaranteed to make you think and bring levity and laughter to your day.

86. TRUE NORTH

True North, the initiative, is an activity that represents living a value-based life and the pursuit of purpose. As a facilitator, challenge your group to form an arrow in the direction they believe to be True North. Give the group 60 seconds, without talking, to accomplish the task. Have the team process what it means to seek out True North. Finding True North is accomplished by using your internal and external compass. We must prepare and create passion about achieving desired end results. We must develop and maintain a healthy body, mind and spirit as we cultivate healthy relationships.

87. SCAN THE GROUP

Be creative in employing many ways to gather feedback from the people you are leading, coaching, facilitating or teaching. Use visual, auditory and kinesthetic methods to be fully aware of the state people are in.

88. TALISMAN

A talisman is an icon or object used for locking in a specific meaning or state — or may even represent magical powers.

89. FINANCIAL LITERACY

In the process of Seeking True North in your personal life and professional organization, it is vital to continue learning more and more in the realm of money. Money is a powerful force on planet

Earth. We would all do well to have an abundance of money and joyfully manage it in productive, positive use for God, others and ourselves.

90. LIFE COMPASS

Purchase a compass and keep it with you at all times. Let it remind you of your need to know your direction in life. Use it as a reference to the bearings of healthy body, mind, spirit and relationships while preparing, practicing and staying passionate about achieving your desired end results.

91. GPS DEVICES

Using a global positioning system (GPS) in a city or nature setting is a great, fun leadership event. Individuals learn many team and leadership tools as well as how to use the GPS system. There can be many complexities to this activity, so contact us for additional information.

92. BUILDING TRUST

There are many activities specifically designed for building trust such as trust traps, physics lean, trust me-trust you and mass-distwuction. Trust is a foundational element in all relationships.

93. IDENTIFYING ANIMAL FECES AND TRACKS

Explore nature and all of its attributes!

94. BALANCING ROCKS

"Balancing rocks" is an intriguing activity performed outside. The process of balancing rocks is very relaxing and rewarding. This activity is particularly good for processing a balanced life in health and wellness and in relationships. The challenge is to balance three rocks on top of each other. However, the rocks should be balanced so that the smaller side of the rock is facing down. Size and shape is up to you, but always keep safety in mind. This is great to do with a partner.

95. RAPPELLING

Rappelling and other ropes-course-type activities provide an outstanding metaphor for trusting systems and stepping into the growth zone. To ensure that any technical ropes course or rappelling initiatives are safe, make sure they are facilitated by qualified people.

96. CLIMBING MYSELF MOUNTAIN

Without a doubt, the most difficult challenges in life come from climbing our own mountains of fears and boldness, irresponsibility and responsibility, self-delusion and integrity, dishonesty and honesty, pride and humility, imbalance and balance. Part of Seeking True North is adjusting our compasses as we align beliefs and values to guide us to our desired end results. Along the way, there will be many storms on this mountain, which sometimes bring disorientation and confusion. Remember that the biggest storms of life also present the opportunity to learn the most. Thankfully, we have so many valuable tools to assist us in this climb!

97. ACCEPTANCE

Acceptance, in spirituality, mindfulness and human psychology, usually refers to the experience of a situation without intention to change that situation. Acceptance does not require that change is possible or even conceivable, nor does it require that the situation be desired or approved by those accepting it. Indeed, acceptance is often suggested when a situation is both disliked and unchangeable, or when change may be possible only at great cost or risk.

98. YODA FACTOR

It takes a confident belief system to achieve the things we desire in life. Consider this scene from *The Empire Strikes Back*:

Luke: All right, I'll give it a try.

Yoda: No. Try not. Do... or do not. There is no try.

[Using the Force, Yoda effortlessly frees Luke's X-Wing ship from the bog]

Luke: I don't…don't believe it.

Yoda: That is why you fail.

99. VARYING PARTNERS

In a group setting, it is important at times to mix people together to build stronger team awareness. The entire team benefits when individuals get to know each other a little better. There are many ways of getting people to interact.

100. TWO TRUTHS AND ONE LIE

The activity we call Two Truths and One Lie provides a great way to get to know others in the group. Each person tells three bits of information about themselves, one of which is a lie. The group then tries to guess which is the lie.

101. BOUNDARIES

We must learn and practice saying "no." We must learn and practice setting boundaries in our lives. And we must be ready to take action in an instant and stand firm. Remember that saying no to one thing is saying yes to something else.

102. THREE CHOICES

This framework provides a simple way to look at any situation: Remove yourself, change it or fully embrace it. Consider your options, choose one and go with it.

103. THE LAW OF ATTRACTION

We attract everything we receive in life. What we attract is what we focus on. When you start focusing on what you want instead of what you don't want, the universe will respond. As we shift our focus to what we do want, we create energy toward receiving. Remember to ask, believe and receive.

104. WOUNDED HEALER

Think of the ways you have been hurt or wounded in your life. Now take that experience and use it to help the many others who have been wounded in the same way you have. We all need a friend with a listening and understanding heart.

105. THE SEVEN MOST IMPORTANT THINGS

Your goal is to list the seven most important things you must do today, in the most effective order of importance. Then do it! Get all of the people around you using this tool as well. It is one of the most powerful and simple time management tools we know of.

106. MATCHING VISUAL, AUDITORY AND KINESTHETIC (VAK) COMMUNICATION STYLES

This communication style tool is a very powerful system of influence to accomplish your desired end results. The goal here is to become proficient in recognizing another's language style and to match your communication responses to that style. With practice, you can shift your style at will to match another's style.

107. CROSS A RIVER

This is another nature-based activity, in which the participants build a pathway across a safe body of water. Many metaphors and learning concepts can be applied in this initiative.

108. GRIP MODEL

The GRIP model is similar in process and provides a framework for diagnosing and increasing team effectiveness and efficiency. The model is hierarchical and starts with goals. The model then directs focus on how the team allocates roles and workloads. Next, the team identifies agreed-upon operating boundaries, styles and cultural issues. Finally, the team addresses process and procedural issues, where effectiveness and efficiency can be defined, benchmarked and refined.

G   *Goal* clarity and commitment are developed.

R   *Roles* define clear areas of responsibility and accountability.

I   *Interpersonal* interactions and relations are explicitly defined to create operating principles.

P   *Process* and procedures are delineated for monitoring and maintaining progress toward an objective.

109. CELEBRATION AND FUN

Make it a habit to celebrate and have fun. Give yourself, and those around you, permission to have more fun and celebrate at right moments. "Bumblebee Tuna!"

110. GENERALIZED PRINCIPLES IN NATURE

The laws and ways of nature can provide many powerful learning metaphors. As stated in the book, seek ideas in nature that can be converted into our realm of human potential.

111. DAMPER SONG

The leader teaches the group the following lyrics and corresponding motions

Lyrics	Motion
Oh you push the damper in	Pump your fist away
And you pull the damper out	Pull your fist in
And the smoke goes up the chimney just the same	Point to the sky and rotate your index finger
Just the same	Tickle the neighbor to your right
Just the same	Tickle the neighbor to your left
And the smoke goes up the chimney just the same	Point to the sky and rotate your index finger

Once the group has the lyrics and motions, sing the song a few more times, gradually substituting the motions for the lyrics each time you sing it, while people laugh hysterically

Oh you… (Pump your fist away)

And you…(Pull your fist in motion)

And the …(Point to the sky and rotate your index finger.)

Etc.

This is a hilarious song for any group to engage in tight quarters… long bus rides are perfect!

112. LEADERSHIP QUOTES

Have each member of the group choose a few favorite inspirational leadership quotes to share with the group. This can be done at one specific time, such as a long bus ride, or scattered throughout a shared experience at various moments.

113. ACTION PLANNING

There are many systems used for action planning. The common denominator is that a specific plan is used to take action toward a specific objective. One powerful way to reinforce the action plans is to create accountability partners. This is where you commit your action plan to another person and agree to check in with each other on your progress together. Create your action plan and get moving!

114. STORYBOARDING

Storyboarding is a powerful tool that involves brainstorming ideas around a given topic and then funneling those ideas into specific action plans. This is a fun, powerful, interactive planning process.

115. SMART GOALS

Goal-setting is a critical part of achieving what you want in life. Many times, we won't achieve something because we haven't clearly defined what we are wanting. The SMART goal system addresses these issues by providing us with a clear method for setting and achieving desired results in our lives. When using the SMART goal-setting system, make sure it has the following elements:

S   *Specific*: The more detailed you are with your goal, the more likely you will be able to achieve it.

M   *Measurable*: Make your goal measurable and you will know whether you have achieved it.

A   *Action-Oriented*: The goal needs to be achieved through some sort of action that is to be taken.

R   *Realistic*: This involves setting your sights on something that you will actually achieve in your chosen timeframe.

T   *Timely*: This indicates when you are aiming to achieve your goal.

116. SELF-ADDRESSED LETTER

Writing a letter to yourself to be mailed later is a great reminder of the goals you set and the focus you desire. You can also write postcards to yourself as you travel to serve as reminders when you return home.

117. ACCOUNTABILITY PARTNERS

An accountability partner is anyone with whom you share your goals in an effort to keep each other on track. Set specific dates with your accountability partner, which will provide a method to monitor each other's progress.

118. LIE, CHEAT AND STEAL

A play on words, which is used just as the Younger Facilitator uses it in the story: "*Lie* in bed at night and consider all the possibilities that life might bring. *Cheat* death by living life with passion every second of every minute of every day. And *steal* away five minutes of your hectic schedule to share an act of kindness with your fellow human beings."

119. THE CHALLENGE

As we stated earlier, our world desperately needs strong leaders. Challenge others to go out and lead. Moreover, challenge them to then challenge others to do the same.

120. COMPASS

The compass is a powerful tool. It can also be a powerful psychological anchor for Seeking True North in our lives. Keep your compass with you and give a compass to a friend.

Afterward

Begin the lifelong pursuit of adding new tools to the list we have started for you. It's up to you to continue gathering more tools and skills to prepare, practice and be passionate about as you continue seeking and living True North. Remember to document your success along the way!

Check our web site for additional resources:
www.SeekingTrueNorth.com

Notes

Notes

Bibliography

Argyris, Chris (1993) *Knowledge for Action. A Guide to Overcoming Barriers to Organizational Change*. San Francisco, California: Jossey-Bass.

Bandler, Richard, and John Grinder (1979) *Frogs Into Princes*. Utah: Real People Press

Bar-On, R. (1997). *Emotional Quotient Inventory (EQ i): Technical Manual*. Canada: Multi-Health Systems.

Bhajan, Yogi, and Gurucharan Khalsa (2000). *Breathwalk: Breathing Your Way to a Revitalized Body, Mind, and Spirit*. New York, New York: Broadway Books.

Blanchard Ph. D., Ken; & Johnson Ph. D., Spencer (1981) *The One Minute Manager*. New York, New York: HarperCollins.

Byrne, R. (Director). (2005). *The Secret* [Motion Picture].

Canfield, J., & Victor Hansen, M. (1995). *The Alladin Factor*. USA: Penguin Group.

Canfield, Jack (2005). *Success Principles: How to Get From Where Are to Where You Want to Be*. New York, New York: HarperCollins Publishers.

Cohen, N. T. (2002). *The Leadership Engine: How Winning Companies Build Leaders at Every Level*. New York, New York: HarperCollins.

Covey, Stephen R. (1989). *The Seven Habits of Highly Effective People*. New York, New York: Simon & Shuster.

Frankl, V. E. (1984). *Man's Search for Meaning* (Third Edition ed.). New York, New York: Simon & Schuster.

Fulsaas, S. M. (2003). *Mountaineering: The Freedom of the Hills* (Edition 7 ed.). Seattle, Washington: The Mountaineers Books.

Gass, Michael P. (1995). *Book of Metaphors* (Vol. II). Dubuque, Iowa: Kendall/Hunt.

Gass, S. P. (1997). *Effective Leadership in Adventure*. Champaign, Illinois: Human Kinetics.

Goleman, C. C. (2001). T*he Emotionally Intelligent Workplace: How to Select for, Measure, and Improve Emotional Intelligence in Individuals, Groups, and Organizations*. San Francisco, California: Josey Bass.

Goleman, D. (1998). *Emotional Intelligence: Why It Can Matter More Than IQ*. New York, New York: Bantam Books.

Handley, R. (1999). *Optimizing People: A Practical Guide for Applying Emotional Intelligence*. New Braunfels, Texas: Profiles-Press.

Hansen, M. V. & Allen, Robert (2002). *The One Minute Millionaire: The Enlightened Way to Wealth*. New York, New York: Harmony Books.

Helmsteader, Shad (1982). *What To Say When You Talk To Yourself*. New York, New York: Pocket Books.

Hill, Napolean (1983) *Think & Grow Rich*. Charleston, South Carolina: Ballantine Books.

Howell, W. S. (1982). *The Empathic Communicator*. Belmont, California: Wadsworth Publishing Company.

Ilgner, A. (2006). *The Rock Warrior's Way: Mental Training for Climbers*. (J. Achey, Ed.) La Vergne, Tennessee: Desiderata Institute.

John E. Sarno, M. (1991). *Healing Back Pain: The Mind-Body Connection*. New York, New York: Warner Books, Inc.

Jones, Charles "Tremendous" (1968). *Life is Tremendous*. Mechanicsburg, Pennsylvania: Executive Books.

Lasseter, J. (Director). (1995). *Toy Story: The Movie* [Motion Picture].

Leahy, T. (1999). National Challenge Course Practitioners Symposium. *Tools from the NCCPS*. Colorado: Leahy, Inc.

Lorayne, Harry (1990). *Memory Power*. New York, New York: Madison Books.

McGee, Robert (1998). *The Search for Significance*. Nashville, Tennessee: W Publishing Group.

Mittleman, S., & Callan, K. (2001). *Slow Burn: Slow Down, Burn Fat, and Unlock the Energy Within*. Harper Collins.

Peter M. Senge, A. K. (1994). *The Fifth Discipline Fieldbook: Strategies and Tools for Building a Learning Organization*. New York, New York: Doubleday.

Peters, Tom (2006). *In Search of Excellence*. New York, New York: Harper Business.

Phillips, D. T. (1992). *Lincoln on Leadership: Executive Strategies for Tough Times*. New York, New York: Time Warner.

Phillips, J. J. (1997). *Return on Investment in Training and Performance Improvement Programs.* Houston, Texas: Gulf Publishing Company.

Poe, Richard (2001). *Wave 3: The New Era in Network Marketing.* Roseville, California: Prima Publishing.

Robbins, Anthony (2003). *Unlimited Power: The New Science of Personal Achievement.* New York, New York: Simon & Schuster.

Rohnke, K. (1984). *Silver Bullets: A Guide to Initiative Problems, Adventure Games, and Trust Activities.* Dubuque, Iowa: Project Adventure.

Rosenthal, R. & Jacobsen, L. (1992). *Pygmalion in the Classroom.* New York, New York: Irvington.

Schoel, Jim (1988). *Islands of Healing.* Hamilton, Massachusetts: Project Adventure Incorporated.

Senge, P. (1990). *The Fifth Discipline: The Art and Practice of the Learning Organization.* New York, New York: Doubleday/Currency.

Staff, M.-W. (1989). *Webster's Dictionary of English Usage.* Merriam-Webster.

Toastmasters. (2007, May). Retrieved from Toastmasters International: www.toastmasters.org

Tolle, E. (1999). *The Power of Now.* Novato, California: New World Library.

Tracy, Brian (2006). *The Psychology of Selling: Increase Your Sales Faster and Easier Than You Ever Thought Possible.* New York, New York: Nelson Business.

Tracy, Brian (2002). *The Psychology of Achievement: Develop the Top-Achievers Mindset.* Chicago, Illinois: Simon & Schuster Audio.

Work Expectations Profile (2001) Inscape Publishing, Inc., Minneapolis, Minnesota

Ziglar, Zig (1975). *See You At The Top.* Gretna, Louisiana: Pelican Publishing Group.

About the Authors

Erick Erickson and Tim Walther

Erick Erickson

Erick Erickson is the founder of Erick Erickson International. Erick and his team of professionals specialize in keynote inspirational speaking, coaching and leadership development for individuals and for teams around the world.

An avid hiker, nature enthusiast, boogie boarder, rock climber and your average ordinary carpenter, Erick is also the proud father of the two best kids in the Universe.

To learn more about Erick Erickson:
erick@seekingtruenorth.com
P.O. Box 100
Jamesville, New York 13078
www.EricksonInternational.com

Tim Walther

Tim Walther, M.S., peak performance and leadership specialist, is the visionary leader of Grand Dynamics International, a training and development organization based in Jackson Hole, Wyoming. Tim holds a Bachelor of Science degree from Ithaca College in Applied Business Psychology and a Master of Science degree in Experiential Education focused on Leadership Studies and Organizational Development from Minnesota State University.

Tim is an avid rock climber and mountaineer, with notable ascents both nationally and internationally. His passion for mountaineering and all-around outdoor adventure keeps the experiential learning process as the hallmark of Grand Dynamics' services. His integration of business acumen and peak performance strategies makes him a sought-after speaker and an authority on successful experiential leadership implementation.

Tim resides in Jackson Hole, Wyoming and plays daily with his faithful Chocolate Labrador Retriever, Telos.

To learn more about Tim Walther:
tim@seekingtruenorth.com
PO Box 6761
Jackson Hole, Wyoming 83002
www.granddynamics.com

Alphabetical Tools Index

www.SeekingTrueNorth.com

Embrace each moment of life and be a being filled with purpose, freedom, beauty and success.

Many of our friends are using the Seeking True North web site forum and blog to share wonderful and inspirational stories and insights. This is a place where you can see, tell and get a sense for how specific tools are working. Please join all of us on the web and at one of our seminars as we seek to explore and embrace all the fantastic models, methods, tools and habits available to us.

We are honored to join you in making a positive difference in our world.

Tim & Erick